Winning Recipes

HEALTHY EATING FOR HEALTHY LIFESTYLES

D1305763

Pictured on the front cover

Black Bean Stir-Fry on pasta, page 120

Winning Recipes

by
PrintWest Publishing Services

Third Printing – October 1998

Copyright © 1998 by
PrintWest Publishing Services
1150 Eighth Avenue
Regina, Saskatchewan
Canada S4R 1C9

Canadian Cataloguing in Publication Data

Main entry under title:

Winning Recipes

Includes index.

ISBN 1-894022-18-1

1. Cookery.

TX714.W56 1998   641.5   C98-920061-2

Photography by: Patricia Holdsworth, Patricia Holdsworth Photography,
Regina, Saskatchewan

Cover Design: Brian Danchuk, Brian Danchuk Design, Regina, Saskatchewan

Tableware courtesy of:
The Compleat Kitchen, Toronto, Ontario
Takumi Company Ltd., Richmond Hill, Ontario

Recipe Development: LeeAnn Bodnaryk
Recipe Testing: Food Focus Saskatoon, Inc.
(Barbara Kovitch, Mary Orr, Linda Braun, Janice Henriksen)
Menu Plans: Rosalie Wynne
Nutrient Analysis: Christina Lengyel, Heather Dzioba, Lisa Carter

Designed, Printed and Produced in Canada by:
Centax Books, a Division of PrintWest Communications Ltd.
Publishing Director, Photo Designer & Food Stylist: Margo Embury
1150 Eighth Avenue, Regina, Saskatchewan, Canada S4R 1C9
(306) 525-2304 FAX: (306) 757-2439

Introduction

Smart eating, healthy eating, good eating – enjoy the delicious full-bodied flavors of *Winning Recipes*. Developed by food professionals these recipes focus on high flavor as well as good nutrition. This array of tempting family-oriented breakfast, lunch and dinner dishes also includes easy-to-make, healthy and portable snack ideas. Healthy food can be comfort food! Savor the wonderful aromas of baking muffins, simmering stews and pasta sauces, sizzling stir-fries. Old-fashioned, family-favorite recipes are updated and exciting new food ideas provide no-fuss, appetizing flavors. High-fiber, nutrition-intense foods include crunchy whole-grain breads, satisfying legume soups, gutsy vegetable combinations and refreshing fruit desserts. Nutritional analysis for all of these flavor-first recipes helps us to eat well, eat smart, so we all win.

Winning Recipes is designed for the entire family. Recipes use readily available fresh ingredients, with some convenience ingredients given for your busiest days. Sample menus provide eight varied eating plans for every day and for special occasions. An International menu and a Vegetarian menu are included, plus A-Day-Away menu and a Just-For-Fun Menu. Sports nutrition information and diabetic meal planning information are also included.

Generous sections on portable lunches and snacks are special features, ideal for families with children and/or parents who take lunches to school, to work or sports events, and want to take healthy, energy-rich snacks to the pool, the track or on hiking and camping trips.

Winning Recipes brings you healthy eating for your and your family's healthy lifestyles.

These recipes have been tested in both metric and U.S. Standard measurement.

Nutrient Analysis:

These recipes were analyzed with Nutritionist IV, Version 4.1 (First DataBank, San Bruno CA) using Canadian food values. Recipes were analyzed using the U.S. Standard measurements and are on a per serving basis.

Where options are given in the ingredient list, the nutritional analysis is done using the first ingredient listed. Variations and serve with suggestions have not been analyzed.

Except where olive oil is specified, canola oil was used in the nutritional analysis throughout.

Sports Nutrition

Sports Nutrition is a relatively new area of studies that applies nutrition principles to enhance sport performance. Some examples of this in practice would be losing excess body fat to enhance efficiency of motion in sport, consuming a high carbohydrate diet to ensure easily accessible energy stores to prevent psychological and physical fatigue, or adequate iron to ensure proper oxygen delivery to the muscles.

The purpose of the food we eat is to provide us with nutrients. The six main classes of nutrients are vitamins, minerals, water, carbohydrate, protein and fat. These nutrients do three things in our body; they provide energy, build and repair body tissues and regulate body processes. Therefore, nutrients are important to everyone, but in the athlete who may have metabolic activity ten times as high as a sedentary person, having these nutrients, and having them in the correct proportion, is increasingly important.

Several studies have shown that physical performance may be seriously hampered by inadequate nutrition. On the other hand, supplemental feedings of nutrients beyond the recommended dietary levels has not been shown to increase physical performance capacity.

Supplements may be considered in certain situations. For example, calcium for those people who don't drink milk, or iron for menstruating women at risk for anemia; but these nutrients should supplement a healthy diet and not be a substitute for one. A physician, dietitian or pharmacist should be consulted before introducing supplements into the diet. These nutrients are best supplied by food because they are found in proportions that our body has evolved to digest and absorb most efficiently.

You may be wondering "What should I eat to optimize my athletic performance?" There isn't a simple answer to this question. Nutrition is affected by gender, age, body weight status, eating and lifestyle patterns, environment, type of training, and the type of sport being participated in. For example, the needs of a weightlifter would be different from those of a marathon runner. Specific dietary modifications may be considered individually, but a nutritionally balanced diet high in carbohydrate is still the cornerstone of good sport nutrition.

The easiest way to ensure that all of the necessary nutrients are eaten is to follow the Food Guide to Healthy Eating. The food guide groups food according to similar nutrient content. Eating a wide variety of foods from all of the groups will help guarantee that all of the nutritional requirements are met.

Table of Contents

Food Guide to Healthy Eating

(For People Four Years and Over) **Different People Need Different Amounts of Food:** The amount of food you need every day from the 4 food groups and other foods depends on your age, body size, activity level, whether you are male or female and if you are pregnant or breast-feeding. That's why the Food Guide gives a lower and higher number of servings for each food group, e.g., young children can choose the lower number of servings, while male teenagers can go to the higher number. Most other people can choose servings somewhere in between.

GRAIN PRODUCTS
5 to 12 Servings per day

1 Serving: 1 slice of toast; 1 oz. (30 g) cold cereal; ¾ cup(175 mL) hot cereal

2 Servings: 1 bagel, pita or bun; 1 cup (250 mL) pasta or rice

VEGETABLES & FRUIT
5 to 10 Servings per day

1 Serving: 1 medium-size vegetable or fruit; ½ cup (125 mL) fresh, frozen or canned vegetables or fruit; 1 cup (250 mL) salad; ½ cup (125 mL) juice

MILK PRODUCTS
5 to 10 Servings per day

1 Serving: 1 cup (250 mL) milk; 1 x 1 x 3" (50 g) cheese; 2 (50 g) cheese slices; ¾ cup (175 mL) yogurt

MEAT/ALTERNATIVES
2 to 3 Servings per day

1 Serving 50-100 g meat. poultry or fish; 1 to 2 eggs; ⅓-⅔ can (50-100 g) canned fish; ⅓ cup (100 g) cheese ½-1 cup (125-250 mL) beans; 2 tbsp. (30 mL) peanut butter;

OTHER FOODS: Taste and enjoyment can also come from foods and beverages not part of the 4 food groups, e.g., snack foods. Some are higher in fat or calories, so use these foods in moderation.

Enjoy a variety of foods from each group every day. Choose lower-fat foods more often.
Grains: Choose whole-grain and enriched products more often.
Vegetables & Fruit: Choose dark green and orange vegetables and orange fruit more often.
Milk Products: Choose lower-fat milk products more often.
Meat/Alternatives: Choose leaner meats, poultry and fish, as well as dried peas, beans and lentils more often.

ANY DAY MENU #1

Breakfast:
Fresh Fruit Frappé, page 12, OR
Mocha Banana Shake, page 13
Bran Muffin, page 27
Milk

Lunch:
Turkey Sausage and Vegetable
  Stew with Cheese Roll
  Topping, page 162
Strawberry Salad with Poppy Seed
  Honey Yogurt Dressing, page 50
Whole-Grain Bread/Buns

Snack:
Cheddar-Stuffed Apple, page 80
Milk/Juice
Whole-Grain Bread/Buns

Dinner:
Bruschetta, page 110
Veal Lasagne with Béchamel Sauce,
  page 134
Broccoli Corn Salad, page 54
Fruit Pizza, page 189
Whole-Grain Bread/Bun

Evening Snack:
Zesty Zucchini Citrus Muffins,
  page 30
Milk/Juice

Grains: 7-8	F&V: 10-11
MP: 3-4	M&A: 2

ANY DAY MENU #2

Breakfast:
Potato Pancakes, page 19
Warm Berry Sauce, page 202
Whole-Grain Toast
Eggs if desired
Milk/Juice

Lunch:
Alphabet Tomato Soup, page
Turkey Sub with Honey Mustard
  Mayo, page 58
Baked Pineapple Sundae, page 193
Milk/Juice

Snack:
Stewed Fruit, page 15
Breakfast Squares, page 25

Dinner:
Broiled Vegetable Salad, page 55
  with Sourdough Bread
Marinated Broiled Lamb Chops,
  page 165
Cheese and Herb Mashed Potatoes,
  page 115
Baked Apples with Apricots,
  page 197

Snack:
Tortilla Spirals, page 107
Milk/Yogurt/Juice
Whole-Grain Bread/Buns

Grains: 8-9	F&V: 8-9
MP: 2-4	M&A: 2-3

F & V – Fruits & Vegetables
MP – Milk Products
M&A – Meat & Alternatives

ANY DAY MENU #3

Breakfast:
Breakfast Roll Ups, page 20
Creamy Orange Shake, page 13
Milk or Yogurt

Lunch:
Broiled Tuna and Egg Bagel, page 63
Broccoli Corn Salad, page 54
Blueberry Banana Whip, page 192

Snack:
Granola, page 85
Milk/Juice

Dinner:
Stuffed Baked Peppers, page 172
Tomato and Mushroom Salad,
 page 53
Steamed Vegetables
Whole-Grain Bread/Bun

Evening Snack:
Fruit and Almond Muffin, page 28
Milk/Juice

Grains: 6-7	F&V: 6-10
MP: 1-3	M&A: 3

ANY DAY MENU #4

Breakfast:
Ham and Swiss Quiche with
 Mushrooms, page 68
Fresh Fruit
Toast
Milk/Juice

Lunch:
Lentil Nachos, page 111
Chunky Chili Stew, page 176
Whole-Grain Bread/Biscuit

Snack:
Strawberry Cheese Dip, page 100,
 with Pound Cake OR
Currant and Walnut Scones, page 24

Dinner:
Beef and Pepper Quesadillas,
 page 182
Chicken in Roasted Red Pepper
 Sauce, page 150
Strawberry Salad with Poppy Seed
 Honey Yogurt Dressing, page 50
Stuffed Plums with Ricotta Cheese,
 page 186
Whole-Grain Bread/Bun

Grains: 7-8	F&V: 9-10
MP: 1-2	M&A: 2-4

The number of servings per menu are suitable for active lifestyles. The menus are meant only as suggestions and in cases where the menus may be in excess or fall short of the daily number of servings of some groups, simply adjust to suit your activity level.

INTERNATIONAL MENU

Breakfast:
Morning Margaritas, page 12
Ham and Swiss Quiche with
  Mushrooms, page 68
Toast

Lunch:
Stuffed Celery Sticks, page 80
Greek Baked Fish, page 140
Pilaf (with vegetables), page 114
Cool Cucumber Salad, page 49
Fruit Kabobs, page 81
Whole-Grain Bread/Buns

Snack:
Fruit and Nut Bagel, page 84
Milk/Juice

Dinner:
Apple, Grape and Cheddar Salad,
  page 49
Layered Italian Meat Loaf, page 174
Broccoli, Mushroom and Tortellini in
  Creamy Garlic Sauce, page 122
Candied Orange Peel on Vanilla
  Frozen Yogurt, page 82
Whole-Grain Bread/Buns

Evening Snack:
Cardamom Prune Cake, page 34
Milk/Juice

Grains: 6-7		F&V: 8-10	
MP: 1-3		M&A: 2-3	

F & V – Fruits & Vegetables
MP – Milk Products
M&A – Meat & Alternatives

VEGETARIAN MENU

(includes milk products and eggs)

Breakfast:
Potato Onion Scramble (omit corned
  beef and substitute with a legume if
  desired), page 16
Banana Bread Slice, page 31
Fresh Fruit

Lunch:
Black Bean Stir-Fry, page 120
Steamed Brown and Wild Rice
Cool Cucumber Salad, page 49
Mango-Pineapple Sorbet, page 187

Snack:
Energy Nuggets, page 91
Milk/Yogurt
Whole-Grain Bun

Dinner:
Mushroom Burgers, page 61
Whole-Grain Bun
Broccoli and Cheddar Stuffed
  Potatoes, page 117
Back-to-Basics Salad, page 46
Milk/Juice

Evening Snack:
Currant and Walnut Scone, page 24
Milk/Juice

Grains: 8-9		F&V: 7-8	
MP: 2-3		M&A: 2-3	

A DAY AWAY MENU

(Note: Refrigeration is necessary to maintain food safety.)

Breakfast:
Banana Bread (2 slices), page 31
Fresh Fruit
Yogurt/Milk

Lunch:
Chef's Salad to Go, page 57
Curried Beef Packet (serve cold/hot), page 78
Dried Fruit and Oat Squares, page 93

Snack:
Berry Nutrition Bars, page 92
Milk/Juice

Dinner:
Autumn Soup (delicious cold or hot in vacuum bottle), page 39
Potato Biscuits, page 23
Hamburger Cups (serve cold or hot), page 72
Fresh Vegetable Selection

Evening Snack:
Cranberry-Orange Muffins, page 29
Juice/Milk

Grains: 7	**F&V:** 9-11
MP: 1-3	**M&A:** 3-4

JUST FOR FUN MENU

Breakfast:
Breakfast Banana Split, page 14
Fresh berries and/or sliced strawberries
Toast
Milk/Juice

Lunch:
Mexican Pizza, page 76
Back-to-Basics Salad, page 46
Crispy Potato Wedges, page 116
Whole-Grain Bread/Buns

Snack:
Orange-Berry Parfait, page 188
"Whatever" Cookies, page 94
Milk/Juice

Dinner:
Ginger Beef Kabobs, page 181
Baby Greens with Fresh Lemon Dressing, page 45
Prawn and Asparagus Fettuccine, page 103
Whole-Grain Bread/Buns

Evening Snack:
Cream of Wheat Cake, page 32
Milk

Grains: 6-7	**F&V:** 7-8
MP: 2-3	**M&A:** 3-4

USING THE NUTRIENT ANALYSIS FOR DIABETIC MEAL PLANNING

Included with the recipes in this book are detailed nutritional analysis for energy (calories), carbohydrates, proteins, fats (further broken down) and vitamins and minerals.

Diabetic exchanges are not included because of the variety of systems for defining "exchanges" or "choices". For those people wishing to fit a recipe into a diabetic meal plan or any other meal plan, information obtained from the nutrient analysis can be used to calculate the food group choices for their particular exchange system.

For example, using the food grouping system described in the "Good Health Eating Guide" produced by the Canadian Diabetes Association, each choice from the:

"Starch Foods" choice contains 15 grams carbohydrate, 2 grams protein and provides about 68 calories;

"Fruits and Vegetables" choice: 10 g carbohydrate, 1 g protein and 44 calories;

"Milk" choice (1% M.F.): 6 g carbohydrate, 4 g protein, 1 g fat and 49 calories (per ½ cup [250 mL] cup);

"Protein Foods" choice: 7 g protein, 3 g fat and 55 calories;

"Fats and Oils" choice: 5 g fat;

"Sugars" choice: 10 g carbohydrate; and

"Extras" choice: no more than 2.5 g carbohydrate.

The analysis of the **Ginger Beef Kebobs** indicates each serving contains:

Calories	241
Protein	21.2 g
Carbohydrate	22.8 g
Fat	7.2 g

This will translate to:

1 starch choice:	15 g carbohydrate	+2 g protein	+ 0 g fat	(68 calories)
2 protein choice:	0 g carbohydrate	+ 14 g protein	+ 6 g fat	(110 calories)
1 milk choice:	6 g carbohydrate	+ 4 g protein	+ 1 g fat	(49 calories)
1 extra choice:	2.5 g carbohydrate	+ 0 g protein	+ 0 g fat	(14 calories)
Total:	23.5 g carbohydrate	+ 20 g protein	+ 7 g fat	(241 calories)

The analysis of the **Banana Bread** indicates each serving (1 slice) contains:

Calories	151
Protein	3.7 g
Carbohydrate	21.4 g
Fat	6.1 g

This will translate to:

½ protein choice:	0 g carbohydrate	+3.5 g protein	+ 1.5 g fat	(27 calories)
2 sugar choices:	20 g carbohydrate	+ 0 g protein	+ 0 g fat	(80 calories)
1 fats choice:	0 g carbohydrate	+ 0 g protein	+ 5 g fat	(45 calories)
Total:	20 g carbohydrate	+ 3.5 g protein	+ 6.5 g fat	(152 calories)

For further information consult your dietician, diabetes nutrition educator, physician or local Diabetes chapter.

Similarly, the nutrient analysis includes components that allow the recipes to be included in other meal plans. The information may assist in meal planning for cardiac diets, renal diets, weight loss/gain and some nutrient deficiencies.

BREAKFASTS & BREADS

HEALTHY EATING FOR HEALTHY LIFESTYLES

Morning Margaritas

A fresh fruit drink for every day or for a special occasion.

4 cups	fresh strawberries*, rinsed, dried and hulled	1 L
1	banana	1
	juice of 1 lime	
3 tbsp.	liquid honey	50 mL
2 cups	ice cubes	500 mL

- In a blender, combine strawberries, banana, lime juice, honey and ice cubes.
- Use a few short whirls to chop up strawberries, banana and ice cubes. On high speed, blend until thick and slushy.
- Pour into 4 margarita or wide-mouthed glasses.

* Frozen strawberries may also be used. When using frozen berries use 1 cup (250 mL) of water instead of the ice cubes.

Yield: 4 servings

Serving Size:
  1 cup (250 mL)
Preparation Time:
  5 minutes

Nutritional Analysis
per serving

Calories:	122
Protein	1.3 g
Carbohydrate	31.2 g
Fiber	3.4 g
Sugar	26 g
Fat	.7 g
Cholesterol	0 mg
Saturated Fat	.1 g
Mono Fat	.1 g
Poly Fat	.3 g
Folate	33 Ug
Vitamin C	91 mg
Sodium	5 mg
Potassium	381 mg
Iron	1 mg
Calcium	26 mg

Fresh Fruit Frappé

A refreshing summer cooler, for breakfast or anytime.

2 cups	cubed honeydew melon, ½" (1 cm) cubes	500 mL
1 cup	halved fresh strawberries	250 mL
1	orange, peeled, quartered, seeded	1
1 cup	pineapple juice	250 mL
	mint sprigs	
	ice cubes	

- In a blender, combine honeydew, strawberries, orange, pineapple juice and mint. Fill the rest of the blender container with ice cubes.
- Blend on medium-high to crush ice, then blend on high for 30 seconds.
- Pour into glasses; garnish with fresh mint sprigs.

Yield: 5 servings

Serving Size:
  1 cup (250 mL)
Preparation Time:
  8 minutes

Nutritional Analysis
per serving

Calories	73
Protein	1 g
Carbohydrate	18.3 g
Fiber	1.8 g
Sugar	16.4 g
Fat	.3 g
Cholesterol	0 mg
Saturated Fat	0g
Mono Fat	0 g
Poly Fat	1g
Folate	24 Ug
Vitamin C	58 mg
Sodium	8 mg
Potassium	362 mg
Iron	0 mg
Calcium	25 mg

Creamy Orange Shake

The orange rind adds texture and flavor to this tangy shake.

1	whole orange, washed well, cut into chunks	1
1½ cups	cold unsweetened orange juice	375 mL
2 cups	no-fat mixed citrus OR orange yogurt	500 mL
1 tbsp.	granulated sugar	15 mL
1 tsp.	vanilla	5 mL

- In a blender, combine orange and orange juice.
- Pulsate a few times to grind the orange then change to high speed for 1 minute to liquefy.
- Add yogurt, sugar and vanilla. Blend on medium high for 30 seconds, until well blended and creamy.

Mocha Banana Shake

Cocoa and coffee add a sophisticated lift to the rich smooth banana flavor.

2 cups	skim milk	500 mL
1	ripe banana	1
1 tbsp.	granulated sugar	15 mL
2 tsp.	instant coffee	10 mL
1 tsp.	low-fat cocoa	5 mL

- In a blender, combine milk, banana, sugar, coffee and cocoa.
- Blend on low for 20 seconds to blend well.

Breakfast Banana Split

Fruit, fiber, yogurt and a touch of chocolate for breakfast!
Delicious.

1	large banana	1
⅔ cup	low-fat strawberry yogurt	150 mL
¼ cup	granola	50 mL
2 tsp.	chocolate sundae topping	10 mL
2	strawberries OR fresh cherries	2

- Peel banana, cut in half crosswise, then lengthwise.
- Lay 2 banana quarters in each of 2 dessert bowls.
- Top each with ⅓ cup (75 mL) of yogurt.
- Sprinkle ½ of granola on each.
- Drizzle 2 tsp. (10 mL) of chocolate topping over each and top with a strawberry.

Variations: Top with your favorite fresh fruit in season, e.g., raspberries, blueberries, sliced peaches, nectarines, etc.

Yield: 2 servings
Serving Size: 1 Banana Split
Preparation Time: 3 minutes

Nutrition Tips:

Do you ever get muscle cramps in your legs at night?

One possible cause is not getting enough Calcium and Magnesium in your diet. Try using more dairy products. Also, try cutting down on soft drinks as they contain a large amount of phosphorous which can inhibit Calcium absorption into the body.

Nutritional Analysis
per serving

Calories	169
Protein	4.9 g
Carbohydrate	31.5 g
Fiber	2.7 g
Sugar	18.9 g
Fat	3.4 g
Cholesterol	2.3 mg
Saturated Fat	2.2 g
Mono Fat	.4 g
Poly Fat	.4 g
Folate	23 Ug
Vitamin C	11 mg
Sodium	90 mg
Potassium	388 mg
Iron	1 mg
Calcium	97 mg

Stewed Fruit

Orange juice plumps and adds fresh flavor to your favorite dried fruit.

½ lb.	dried mixed fruit (apple, peach, pear, prune, apricot)	250 g
2 cups	water	500 mL
½ cup	unsweetened orange juice	125 mL
2 tbsp.	granulated sugar	25 mL

- In a medium saucepan, combine fruit, water, orange juice and sugar.
- Heat over medium heat until it comes to a boil.
- Stir and reduce heat to minimum. Cover.
- Simmer slowly for 1 hour.
- Remove from heat.
- Keep covered and cool.
- Store fruit mixture in a sealed container in the refrigerator for up to 1 month.

Serve with toast or toasted bagels.

Variations: Try adding dried blueberries or cranberries, or substituting other juices for the orange juice.

Yield: 8 servings
Serving Size: ½ cup (125 mL)
Preparation Time: 5 minutes

Nutritional Analysis
per serving

Calories	94
Protein	.9 g
Carbohydrate	24.7 g
Fiber	2 g
Sugar	19.9 g
Fat	.1 g
Cholesterol	0 mg
Saturated Fat	0 g
Mono Fat	.1 g
Poly Fat	0 g
Folate	9 Ug
Vitamin C	7 mg
Sodium	4 mg
Potassium	273 mg
Iron	1 mg
Calcium	15 mg

Nutrition Tips:

To renew your energy reserves, start your day with a balanced breakfast. Milk (milk or yogurt), Grains (cereal, toast or a bagel) and Fruit (juice, a fruit shake or whole fruit) gives you one serving each from three of the four food groups.

Potato Onion Scramble

*This is a great weekend breakfast or brunch dish.
It looks good and the aroma is irresistible.*

2 tbsp.	butter	25 mL
1	medium onion, diced	1
2 cups	grated raw potato	500 mL
½ cup	water	125 mL
	salt and black pepper to taste	
½ cup	diced corned beef	125 mL
	(approximately 8-10 thin slices)	
4	eggs	4
½ tsp.	Worcestershire sauce	2 mL
5 drops	Tabasco sauce	5 drops
	chopped green onion OR parsley to garnish	

- Heat a large nonstick frying pan over medium heat and melt butter.
- Add onion, potato, water, salt and pepper; stir well. Cover.
- Reduce heat; simmer for 10 minutes. Remove lid, water should have disappeared and potato should be almost cooked.
- Sprinkle corned beef on top of potato mixture.
- Beat eggs and stir in Worcestershire sauce and Tabasco sauce.
- Pour eggs over potatoes, stir and let set.
- Sprinkle with green onions or parsley. Serve immediately.

Variations: Black Forest ham can be substituted for corned beef. Top with grated Cheddar or Monterey Jack cheese if you wish.

Breakfasts & Breads

Potato Onion Scramble, page 16

Yield: 4 servings
Serving Size: ¾ cup
(175 mL)
Preparation Time:
25 minutes.

Nutritional Analysis
per serving

Calories	222
Protein	12.5 g
Carbohydrate	18.2 g
Fiber	1.8 g
Sugar	2 g
Fat	11.6 g
Cholesterol	240 mg
Saturated Fat	5.4 g
Mono Fat	3.8 g
Poly Fat	1 g
Folate	36 Ug
Vitamin C	18 mg
Sodium	363 mg
Potassium	372 mg
Iron	1 mg
Calcium	38 mg

Potato Pancakes

Potato pancakes are a much-loved comfort food in many countries. Jewish Latkes, Swedish Rarakor, Polish Racuchy, Swiss Rosti, are all delicious versions of potato pancakes.

½ cup	all-purpose flour	125 mL
1 tsp.	salt	5 mL
1 tsp.	baking powder	5 mL
½ tsp.	black pepper	2 mL
1	egg	1
½ cup	1% milk	125 mL
2 tbsp.	butter, melted	25 mL
1¾ cups	grated potato, moisture squeezed out	425 mL
1 tbsp.	grated onion	15 mL
4 tsp.	canola oil, divided	20 mL

- In a bowl, combine flour, salt, baking powder and pepper. Stir well.
- Add egg, milk and butter. Beat for 1 minute with a rotary beater.
- Add potato and onion. Stir well.
- In a large, heavy nonstick frying pan, over medium to medium-low heat, heat 1 tbsp. (15 mL) oil.
- Using a ¼ cup (50 mL) measure, scoop 4 portions of potato batter into the hot frying pan. Flatten to 4" (10 cm) circles.
- Fry for 2½ minutes on each side, until golden brown and potato in the center of the pancake is cooked.
- Remove pancakes, keep warm.
- Add 1 tsp. (5 mL) oil to frying pan. Cook the last 4 pancakes following the same procedure.

Serve with sour cream and/or applesauce.

Yield: 4 servings (8 pancakes)

Serving size: 2 pancakes
Preparation Time:
  15 minutes

Nutritional Analysis
per serving

Calories	300
Protein	6.6 g
Carbohydrate	41.2 g
Fiber	3 g
Sugar	4 g
Fat	12.6 g
Cholesterol	70.6 mg
Saturated Fat	4.8 g
Mono Fat	2.3 g
Poly Fat	1.9 g
Folate	24 Ug
Vitamin C	11 mg
Sodium	772 mg
Potassium	530 mg
Iron	2 mg
Calcium	146 mg

Breakfast Roll Ups

A flavorful new version of bacon and eggs.

4	strips turkey bacon	4
4	eggs	4
2 tbsp.	milk	25 mL
2 tsp.	butter	10 mL
	salt and pepper to taste	
4, 8"	flour tortillas	4, 20 cm

- Cook turkey bacon in microwave or frying pan as per package directions.
- Melt butter in a small nonstick frying pan over medium heat.
- Add eggs and milk. Stir to break yolks. Season with salt and pepper.
- Reduce heat to medium low. Cook until eggs are set, stirring occasionally.
- On High in microwave, on paper towel, heat tortillas 10 seconds each, or warm tortillas in the oven.
- Down the center of each tortilla, lay 1 strip of turkey bacon and ¼ of the eggs. Roll up.
- Rewrap in paper towel if eating on the go.

Variations: Before rolling up, you can add jalapeño (hot pepper) sauce, salsa, chopped onion, grated cheese, etc., to vary flavors.

Yield: 4 servings
Serving Size: 1 roll up
Preparation Time:
  6 minutes

Nutritional Analysis
per serving

Calories	240
Protein	11.6 g
Carbohydrate	20.5 g
Fiber	1.2 g
Sugar	.4 g
Fat	12.2 g
Cholesterol	228 mg
Saturated Fat	3.8 g
Mono Fat	3.5 g
Poly Fat	1.7 g
Folate	28 Ug
Vitamin C	0 mg
Sodium	445 mg
Potassium	119 mg
Iron	2 mg
Calcium	78 mg

French Toast

With warm berry sauce, applesauce, fruit preserves, lemon juice and icing (confectioner's) sugar, fresh berries and liquid honey, brown sugar and cinnamon and butter, or maple syrup, French Toast is a memorable breakfast treat.

2	eggs	2
⅔ cup	1% milk	150 mL
1 tbsp.	granulated sugar	15 mL
½ tsp.	vanilla	2 mL
⅛ tsp.	salt	0.5 mL
2 tbsp.	margarine, divided	25 mL
10, ½"	slices of French bread	10, 1 cm

- In a pie plate, whisk together eggs, milk, sugar, vanilla and salt until well blended.
- Heat a large heavy frying pan over medium to medium-low heat.
- Melt 1 tbsp. (15 mL) margarine.
- Dip each side of bread in egg mixture. Let excess drain back into plate.
- Lay 5 slices at a time in the frying pan. Fry for 1½ minutes, or until golden brown. Turn and cook the other side.
- Keep cooked toast warm in the oven while cooking the second batch, using the 1 tbsp. (15 mL) margarine.

Variations: a dash of cinnamon or grated orange or lemon rind can be added to the milk and egg mixture.

Yield: 5 servings (10 pieces of French Toast)

Serving Size: 2 slices
Preparation Time: 15 minutes

Nutritional Analysis
per serving

Calories	232
Protein	8 g
Carbohydrate	30.5 g
Fiber	1.5 g
Sugar	5.9 g
Fat	8.4 g
Cholesterol	86.1 mg
Saturated Fat	2 g
Mono Fat	3.3 g
Poly Fat	2.4 g
Folate	27 Ug
Vitamin C	0 mg
Sodium	467 mg
Potassium	134 mg
Iron	2 mg
Calcium	89 mg

Poppy Seed Pancakes

½ cup	whole-wheat flour	125 mL
½ cup	oatmeal	125 mL
½ cup	cornmeal	125 mL
1 cup	all-purpose flour	250 mL
1 tbsp.	poppy seeds	15 mL
2 tbsp.	brown sugar	25 mL
2 tsp.	baking powder	10 mL
1 tsp.	baking soda	5 mL
1 tsp.	salt	5 mL
2	eggs	2
¼ cup	canola oil	50 mL
2 cups	buttermilk	500 mL
1 tsp.	vanilla	5 mL
	canola oil	

- In a large bowl, mix together whole-wheat flour, oatmeal, cornmeal, flour, poppy seeds, brown sugar, baking powder, baking soda and salt.
- In a small bowl, beat eggs with a fork until well blended.
- To egg mixture add oil, buttermilk and vanilla. Mix well.
- Add wet mixture to dry. Stir just until all dry ingredients are mixed in. Let rest 5 minutes.
- Heat a large heavy frying pan over medium heat. Lightly wipe the pan with oil.
- Using a ⅓ cup (75 mL) scoop, pour batter into the frying pan. Make 3 pancakes at a time.
- Flip pancakes over when nicely browned, 1 to 1½ minutes. Cook the same on the other side. Heat may have to be reduced if pancakes are browning too quickly on the outside and not fully cooked on the inside. It will depend on how heavy the pan is.

Serve with your favorite topping or Warm Berry Sauce, page 202.

Yield: 4 servings (12 pancakes)
Serving Size: 3, 4"
(10 cm) pancakes
Preparation Time:
20 minutes

Nutritional Analysis
per serving

Calories	495
Protein	14.1 g
Carbohydrate	69.9 g
Fiber	8.2 g
Sugar	13.1 g
Fat	19 g
Cholesterol	106 mg
Saturated Fat	2.1 g
Mono Fat	1.5 g
Poly Fat	5.7 g
Folate	96 Ug
Vitamin C	21 mg
Sodium	1143 mg
Potassium	449 mg
Iron	4 mg
Calcium	271 mg

Potato Biscuits

These are a good way to use up leftover mashed potatoes.
Potato biscuits are very good with soup, stew or chili.
Tightly wrap leftover biscuits for a snack the next day.

1¼ cups	all-purpose flour	300 mL
¼ cup	cornmeal	50 mL
4 tsp.	baking powder	20 mL
½ tsp.	salt	2 mL
1 cup	cold, mashed potatoes	250 mL
¼ cup	shortening	50 mL
⅔ cup	2% milk	150 mL

- Preheat oven to 425°F (220°C).
- In a large bowl, sift together flour, cornmeal, baking powder and salt.
- Add mashed potatoes and shortening. Cut with a knife or pastry blender until thoroughly mixed and texture is crumbly.
- Add milk to make a soft dough. Do not over mix.
- Turn the dough onto a floured surface. Knead for 6 turns.
- Roll the dough to ¾" (2 cm) thick. Cut with a floured 2" (5 cm) round cutter.
- Place biscuits on a baking sheet lightly sprayed with a nonstick cooking spray. Bake the biscuits for 10 to 15 minutes, or until nicely golden.

Pictured on page 177.

Yield: 8 servings (16 biscuits)
Serving Size: 2 biscuits
Preparation Time: 20 minutes

Nutritional Analysis
per serving

Calories	182
Protein	3.6 g
Carbohydrate	24.4 g
Fiber	1.1 g
Sugar	1.5 g
Fat	7.5 g
Cholesterol	1.6 mg
Saturated Fat	1.9 g
Mono Fat	2.7 g
Poly Fat	1.8 g
Folate	10 Ug
Vitamin C	2 mg
Sodium	383 mg
Potassium	138 mg
Iron	1 mg
Calcium	210 mg

Currant and Walnut Scones

2 cups	all-purpose flour	500 mL
2 tbsp.	granulated sugar	25 mL
4 tsp.	baking powder	20 mL
½ tsp.	salt	2 mL
¼ cup	shortening	50 mL
½ cup	currants	125 mL
⅓ cup	chopped walnuts	75 mL
1	egg	1
⅔ cup	1% milk	150 mL
	1% milk for topping	
	granulated sugar for topping	

- Preheat oven to 400°F (200°C).
- In a medium bowl, combine flour, sugar, baking powder and salt.
- With 2 knives, or a pastry blender, cut shortening into dry ingredients until mixture is crumbly.
- Mix in currants and walnuts.
- In a small bowl, lightly beat egg with a fork, whisk in milk.
- Gradually add the milk mixture to the flour mixture. Stir until dough forms a ball.
- On a floured surface, knead dough lightly about 12 times, folding over each time.
- Pat into an 8 to 9" (20 to 22 cm) circle, ½ to ¾" (1 to 1.5 cm) thick. Cut into 8 wedges.
- Brush with milk and sprinkle sugar on top.
- Place on baking sheet and bake for 16 to 20 minutes, until golden brown.

Variations: Substitute chopped pecans or almonds for walnuts if you prefer.

Yield: 8 servings
Serving size: 1 wedge
Preparation time:
  15 minutes

Nutritional Analysis
per serving

Calories	257
Protein	6.3 g
Carbohydrate	35.8 g
Fiber	1.7 g
Sugar	4.6 g
Fat	10.1 g
Cholesterol	27.3 mg
Saturated Fat	2.1 g
Mono Fat	3 g
Poly Fat	3.7 g
Folate	17 Ug
Vitamin C	1 mg
Sodium	347 mg
Potassium	177 mg
Iron	2 mg
Calcium	219 mg

Citrus Apple Breakfast Squares

1 cup	whole-wheat flour	250 mL
¾ cup	natural bran	175 mL
½ cup	rolled oats	125 mL
2 tbsp.	sesame seeds	25 mL
1 tbsp.	grated lemon peel	15 mL
1 tbsp.	grated orange peel	15 mL
1 tsp.	baking powder	5 mL
¼ tsp.	EACH baking soda and salt	1 mL
⅓ cup	soft margarine	75 mL
½ cup	brown sugar, divided	125 mL
1	egg	1
5 tbsp.	fresh lemon juice, divided	75 mL
3 tbsp.	fresh orange juice	45 mL
1	apple, washed, coarsely grated	1
½ cup	chopped raisins	125 mL
½ cup	chopped walnuts (or any nuts)	125 mL
¼ cup	unsweetened medium coconut	50 mL

- Preheat oven to 350°F (180°C).
- In a bowl, combine flour, bran, rolled oats, sesame seeds, lemon peel, orange peel, baking powder, baking soda and salt.
- In another bowl, cream margarine with ¼ cup (50 mL) brown sugar. Add egg and beat until light and fluffy.
- Stir flour mixture into egg mixture, until completely moistened.
- In a medium bowl, combine 3 tbsp. (45 mL) lemon juice, orange juice, apple, raisins, walnuts, ¼ cup (50 mL) brown sugar and coconut.
- Spray an 8 x 8" (20 x 20 cm) pan with a nonstick cooking spray.
- Pat half of the dough mixture into the bottom of the pan. Spread with apple and raisin mixture. Press remaining dough firmly on top.
- Bake for 30 minutes. Remove from the oven. Cool on rack. Cover with foil until the next day.
- Cut into 2 x 2" (5 x 5 cm) squares.

Yield: 16 servings
Serving Size: 1 square, 2 x 2" (5 x 5 cm)
Preparation Time: 22 minutes

Nutritional Analysis
per serving

Calories	176
Protein	3.8 g
Carbohydrate	24.7 g
Fiber	2.7 g
Sugar	12.9 g
Fat	7.9 g
Cholesterol	13.3 mg
Saturated Fat	1.5 g
Mono Fat	2.2 g
Poly Fat	3.1 g
Folate	12 Ug
Vitamin C	5 mg
Sodium	145 mg
Potassium	181 mg
Iron	1 mg
Calcium	46 mg

Savory Sun-Dried Tomato Muffins

1 oz.	sun-dried tomatoes	30 g
½ cup	hot water	125 mL
1½ cups	all-purpose flour	375 mL
¾ cup	whole-wheat flour	175 mL
1 tbsp.	granulated sugar	15 mL
1 tsp.	baking soda	5 mL
2 tsp.	baking powder	10 mL
1 tsp.	salt	5 mL
1 tsp.	dry dillweed	5 mL
¼ cup	finely chopped green onions	50 mL
2 tbsp.	olive oil	25 mL
1	egg	1
1½ cups	plain no-fat yogurt	375 mL

- Preheat oven to 375°F (190°C).
- In a small bowl, rehydrate tomatoes in hot water for 10 minutes. Drain tomatoes and chop.
- Spray a muffin tin with nonstick cooking spray.
- In a large bowl, combine flours, sugar, baking soda, baking powder, salt and dillweed.
- Add tomatoes and green onion. Toss to coat well.
- In another bowl, whisk together olive oil, egg, sugar and yogurt. Add to dry mixture; mix until just moistened.
- Fill muffin cups ¾ full with batter.
- Bake 15 to 18 minutes, or until firm to the touch.
- Remove from pan and serve immediately.

Yield: 12 servings (12 muffins)
Serving Size: 1 muffin
Preparation Time:
15 minutes

Nutritional Analysis
per serving

Calories	136
Protein	5.1 g
Carbohydrate	22.6 g
Fiber	1.5 g
Sugar	3.2 g
Fat	2.9 g
Cholesterol	17.7 mg
Saturated Fat	.5 g
Mono Fat	1.8 g
Poly Fat	.4 g
Folate	14 Ug
Vitamin C	3 mg
Sodium	390 mg
Potassium	163 mg
Iron	1 mg
Calcium	125 mg

Bran Muffins

This muffin batter can be stored in the refrigerator for several days. You can bake muffins in several batches and have them fresh every morning.

2	eggs	2
1 cup	granulated sugar	250 mL
½ cup	canola oil	125 mL
¼ cup	molasses	50 mL
2 cups	1% milk	500 mL
1½ cups	natural bran	375 mL
2 cups	all-purpose flour	500 mL
2 tsp.	baking powder	10 mL
2 tsp.	baking soda	10 mL
1 tsp.	salt	5 mL
1½ cups	raisins	375 mL

- In a large bowl, whisk together eggs, sugar, oil, molasses and milk.
- In another bowl, combine bran, flour, baking powder, baking soda, salt and raisins.
- Combine dry mixture with wet mixture; mix well. Refrigerate for 30 minutes.
- Preheat oven to 325°F (160°C).
- Spoon batter evenly into 18 muffin tins, lightly sprayed with nonstick cooking spray.
- Bake for 20 minutes, or until tops spring back when lightly touched.

Nutrition Tips:

What is "The Burn"?

In high intensity, short-term (1-2 minutes) exercise bouts, not enough oxygen gets to the working muscle. Energy is formed without oxygen by the breakdown of glycogen into lactic acid. This buildup of lactic acid alters the pH of the muscle, causing "the burn".

Yield: 18 servings (18 muffins)
Serving Size: 1 muffin
Preparation Time:
  10 minutes (30 minutes chilling time)

Nutritional Analysis
per serving

Calories	231
Protein	4 g
Carbohydrate	38.7 g
Fiber	1.9 g
Sugar	22.1 g
Fat	7.4 g
Cholesterol	24.6 mg
Saturated Fat	1 g
Mono Fat	.3 g
Poly Fat	2 g
Folate	10 Ug
Vitamin C	1 mg
Sodium	338 mg
Potassium	303 mg
Iron	2 mg
Calcium	113 mg

Fruit and Almond Muffins

2 cups	all-purpose flour	500 mL
⅓ cup	packed brown sugar	75 mL
1 tbsp.	baking powder	15 mL
½ tsp.	baking soda	2 mL
½ tsp.	salt	2 mL
1	egg, beaten	1
1 cup	no-fat any-fruit-flavor yogurt	250 mL
¼ cup	canola oil	50 mL
14 oz.	fruit cocktail in juice drained (reserve ¼ cup [50 mL] of juice)	398 mL
½ tsp.	almond extract	2 mL
	brown sugar	
	flaked natural almonds	

- Preheat oven to 400°F (200°C).
- In a large bowl, mix together flour, brown sugar, baking powder, baking soda and salt.
- Make a well in the center.
- In another bowl combine egg, yogurt, oil, fruit cocktail, reserved juice and almond extract.
- Add the fruit mixture to the flour mixture, all at once.
- Stir just until moistened. Batter should be thick and lumpy.
- Lightly spray muffin tins with nonstick cooking spray.
- Fill muffin cups ⅔ full with batter. Lightly sprinkle the top of each with brown sugar and almonds.
- Bake 20 to 25 minutes, or until a toothpick inserted in the center of a muffin comes out clean.

Yield: 12 servings (12 muffins)
Serving Size: 1 muffin
Preparation Time: 18 minutes

Nutritional Analysis
per serving

Calories	208
Protein	4.3 g
Carbohydrate	33.7 g
Fiber	1.1 g
Sugar	16.3 g
Fat	6.4 g
Cholesterol	18.2 mg
Saturated Fat	.6 g
Mono Fat	.5 g
Poly Fat	1.8 g
Folate	8 Ug
Vitamin C	1 mg
Sodium	263 mg
Potassium	144 mg
Iron	1 mg
Calcium	143 mg

Cranberry-Orange Muffins

2 cups	fresh OR frozen cranberries, coarsely chopped	500 mL
¾ cup	granulated sugar, divided grated rind of 1 orange	175 mL
½ cup	margarine	125 mL
2	eggs	2
1 cup	orange yogurt	250 mL
2½ cups	all-purpose flour	625 mL
2 tsp.	baking powder	10 mL
1 tsp.	baking soda	5 mL
¼ tsp.	salt	1 mL

- Preheat oven to 375°F (190°C).
- In a small bowl, combine chopped cranberries, ¼ cup (50 mL) sugar and orange rind. Set aside.
- In a large bowl, beat, with an electric hand mixer, margarine, ½ cup (125 mL) sugar, eggs and yogurt until blended.
- In another bowl, combine flour, baking powder, baking soda and salt. Add to yogurt mixture along with cranberries. Mix until just blended.
- Lightly spray muffin tins with nonstick cooking spray. Fill tins ⅔ full.
- Bake for 20 minutes, or until golden.

Nutrition Tips:

What does Iron do for us?

This mineral is essential for developing many compounds in the body – an important one is hemoglobin. Hemoglobin is the component of blood that transports oxygen around the body. Males seldom have to worry about iron deficiency, whereas females may have to be careful. Losses through menstruation put females at risk for low iron. This hampers athletic performance and contributes to early fatigue.

Yield: 16 servings (16 muffins)
Serving Size: 1 muffin
Preparation Time:
  15 minutes

Nutritional Analysis
per serving

Calories	189
Protein	3.6 g
Carbohydrate	28.8 g
Fiber	1.1 g
Sugar	11.6 g
Fat	6.7 g
Cholesterol	27.3 mg
Saturated Fat	1.4 g
Mono Fat	2.5 g
Poly Fat	2.4 g
Folate	10 Ug
Vitamin C	2 mg
Sodium	254 mg
Potassium	69 mg
Iron	1 mg
Calcium	75 mg

Zesty Zucchini Citrus Muffins

2	eggs	2
⅓ cup	canola oil	75 mL
1 tsp.	grated lime rind	5 mL
2 tsp.	grated lemon rind	10 mL
2 tsp.	grated orange rind	10 mL
2 tbsp.	fresh orange juice	25 mL
1 tbsp.	fresh lemon juice	15 mL
1 tbsp.	fresh lime juice	15 mL
⅔ cup	granulated sugar	150 mL
1½ cups	grated zucchini	375 mL
2 cups	all-purpose flour	500 mL
2 tsp.	baking powder	10 mL
½ tsp.	baking soda	2 mL
¼ tsp.	salt	1 mL
⅛ tsp.	nutmeg	0.5 mL

Citrus Drizzle

¼ cup	combined fresh lime, lemon and orange juice	50 mL
¼ cup	granulated sugar	50 mL

- Preheat oven to 425°F (220°C).
- In a large bowl, beat together by hand, eggs, oil, lime, lemon and orange rinds, orange, lemon and lime juice, sugar and zucchini.
- In a small bowl, mix flour, baking powder, baking soda, salt and nutmeg.
- Stir flour mixture into the zucchini mixture.
- Lightly spray muffin tins with a nonstick cooking spray. Fill tins ⅔ full.
- Bake for 16 to 18 minutes, or until a toothpick inserted in the center comes out clean.
- To make the drizzle, combine lime, lemon and orange juices with sugar. Stir well.
- Slowly spoon citrus drizzle over muffins. Let cool for 5 minutes. Remove from the tins and cool on a rack.

Yield: 12 servings (12 muffins)
Serving Size: 1 muffin
Preparation Time: 12 minutes

Nutritional Analysis
per serving

Calories	207
Protein	3.5 g
Carbohydrate	33 g
Fiber	.8 g
Sugar	16.4 g
Fat	7.2 g
Cholesterol	35.3 mg
Saturated Fat	.7 g
Mono Fat	.3 g
Poly Fat	2 g
Folate	17 Ug
Vitamin C	5 mg
Sodium	173 mg
Potassium	88 mg
Iron	1 mg
Calcium	67 mg

Banana Bread

Everyone has a favorite recipe for banana bread.
This version has roasted peanuts and flax seed for added
nutrition, texture and flavor.

¼ cup	margarine	50 mL
½ cup	granulated sugar	125 mL
2	eggs	2
1¼ cups	all-purpose flour	300 mL
½ cup	whole-wheat flour	125 mL
¼ cup	natural bran	50 mL
1 tsp.	baking soda	5 mL
½ tsp.	salt	2 mL
3	large ripe bananas, mashed	3
1 tsp.	vanilla	5 mL
½ cup	chopped roasted peanuts	125 mL
¼ cup	flax seed	50 mL

- Preheat oven to 350°F (180°C).
- Lightly grease a 2½ x 5 x 9" (6 x 13 x 23 cm) loaf pan.
- In a large bowl, cream margarine and sugar until light and fluffy.
- Add eggs, 1 at a time, beating well after each.
- Sift all-purpose flour, whole-wheat flour, bran, baking soda and salt. Add to egg mixture.
- Add bananas, vanilla, peanuts and flax seed. Stir lightly until just mixed.
- Turn into prepared loaf pan.
- Bake for 50 to 60 minutes, or until a toothpick inserted in the loaf comes out clean.
- Cool in the pan for 10 minutes. Turn the loaf out onto a cooling rack.

Yield: 18 servings
Serving Size: ½"
 (1 cm) slice
Preparation Time:
 18 minutes

Nutritional Analysis
per serving

Calories	151
Protein	3.7 g
Carbohydrate	21.4 g
Fiber	2 g
Sugar	8.7 g
Fat	6.1 g
Cholesterol	23.6 mg
Saturated Fat	1.1 g
Mono Fat	2.4 g
Poly Fat	2.2 g
Folate	23 Ug
Vitamin C	2 mg
Sodium	211 mg
Potassium	162 mg
Iron	1 mg
Calcium	15 mg

Cream of Wheat Cake

A rich custard-like cake with a very smooth texture, this cake is best made the day before serving. It's very good served with a mug of warm milk or hot chocolate.

½ cup	cream of wheat	125 mL
2 cups	2% milk	500 mL
⅓ cup	margarine OR butter	75 mL
½ cup	granulated sugar	125 mL
1 tsp.	vanilla	5 mL
36	40%-less-fat graham wafers*	36

- Bring cream of wheat and milk to a boil. Reduce heat to low and cook for 3 to 4 minutes, until thickened, stirring occasionally.
- Set aside to cool for 30 minutes, stirring occasionally.
- In a large mixing bowl, cream together margarine, sugar and vanilla with an electric mixer. Add cream of wheat; beat until smooth and thick.
- Line a 7 x 11" (17 x 28 cm) cake pan with 12 graham wafers.
- Spread half the filling on top of wafers. Lay another layer of 12 wafers on top, followed by the other half of the filling, then layer remaining graham wafers on top.
- Cover. Refrigerate until wafers are soft and filling has set. Cut into 12, 2 x 2" (5 x 5 cm) squares.

* You may require more or fewer graham wafers, depending on their size.

Yield: 12 servings
Serving Size: 1 square,
  2 x 2" (5 x 5 cm)
Preparation Time:
  45 minutes

Nutritional Analysis
per serving

Calories	159
Protein	2.2 g
Carbohydrate	20.5 g
Fiber	.1 g
Sugar	13.7 g
Fat	7.6 g
Cholesterol	10.6 mg
Saturated Fat	1.7 g
Mono Fat	2.8 g
Poly Fat	2.3 g
Folate	2 Ug
Vitamin C	0 mg
Sodium	118 mg
Potassium	75 mg
Iron	1 mg
Calcium	58 mg

Rhubarb and Blueberry Coffee Cake

¾ cup	granulated sugar	175 mL
½ cup	margarine, softened	125 mL
2	eggs	2
1 cup	buttermilk	250 mL
1 tsp.	vanilla	5 mL
½ tsp.	almond extract	2 mL
1⅓ cups	all-purpose flour	325 mL
1 cup	whole-wheat flour	250 mL
2 tsp.	baking powder	10 mL
½ tsp.	baking soda	2 mL
¼ tsp.	salt	1 mL
1 cup	blueberries, fresh OR frozen	250 mL
3 cups	chopped rhubarb	750 mL
⅓ cup	sliced almonds	75 mL
⅓ cup	granulated sugar	75 mL
½ tsp.	ground cinnamon	2 mL

- Preheat oven to 350°F (180°C).
- In a large bowl, beat sugar with margarine until light, 1½ minutes.
- Beat in eggs, 1 at a time; beat well after each.
- Beat in buttermilk, vanilla and almond extract.
- In another bowl, stir together flours, baking powder, baking soda and salt.
- Stir in egg mixture, just until blended. Add blueberries; gently fold in.
- Spread into a 9 x 13" (22 x 34 cm) cake pan lightly sprayed with a nonstick cooking spray.
- Sprinkle rhubarb on top.
- In a small bowl, combine almonds, sugar and cinnamon. Sprinkle over rhubarb.
- Bake for 1 hour, or until a toothpick inserted in the center comes out clean.
- Cool in the pan on a rack.
- Cut into 12, 3 x 3" (7.5 x 7.5 cm) squares.

Yield: 12 servings
Serving Size: 1 square,
  3 x 3" (7.5 x 7.5 cm)
Preparation Time:
  22 minutes

Nutritional Analysis
per serving

Calories	278
Protein	5.7 g
Carbohydrate	41.3 g
Fiber	3.5 g
Sugar	20.3 g
Fat	10.7 g
Cholesterol	35.3 mg
Saturated Fat	1.8 g
Mono Fat	4.5 g
Poly Fat	3.8 g
Folate	24 Ug
Vitamin C	8 mg
Sodium	281 mg
Potassium	232 mg
Iron	2 mg
Calcium	118 mg

Cardamom Prune Cake

Great for a quick breakfast with fruit and a glass of milk or to take along for coffee break.

½ cup	margarine, softened	125 mL
1 cup	packed brown sugar	250 mL
2	eggs	2
1¾ cups	all-purpose flour	425 mL
½ tsp.	salt	2 mL
1 tsp.	baking powder	5 mL
1 tsp.	baking soda	5 mL
2 tsp.	cardamom	10 mL
½ tsp.	cinnamon	5 mL
1 cup	buttermilk OR sour milk	250 mL
1 cup	chopped prunes	250 mL

- Lightly spray a 7 x 11" (17 x 28 cm) cake pan with nonstick cooking spray. Sprinkle with flour to coat all sides.
- Preheat oven to 350°F (180°C).
- In a large bowl, cream margarine with brown sugar. Beat in eggs.
- In another bowl, sift flour, salt, baking powder, baking soda, cardamom and cinnamon.
- Add to creamed mixture alternately with buttermilk.
- Mix in prunes.
- Pour batter into prepared cake pan.
- Bake 35 minutes, or until a toothpick inserted in the center comes out clean.
- Let cool on rack.
- Cover cake with foil and let cake ripen until the next day.
- Cut into 15, 2 x 2" (5 x 5 cm) squares.

* To sour milk mix 1 cup (250 mL) milk and 1 tbsp. (15 mL) vinegar or lemon juice. Let sit 5 minutes.

Yield: 15 servings
Serving Size: 1 square,
2 x 2" (5 x 5 cm)
Preparation Time:
18 minutes

Nutritional Analysis
per serving

Calories	200
Protein	3 g
Carbohydrate	32.6 g
Fiber	1.6 g
Sugar	18.4 g
Fat	6.9 g
Cholesterol	28.3 mg
Saturated Fat	1.3 g
Mono Fat	2.7 g
Poly Fat	2.5 g
Folate	15 Ug
Vitamin C	3 mg
Sodium	286 mg
Potassium	179 mg
Iron	1 mg
Calcium	55 mg

Lunches, At Home & Portable

Healthy Eating for Healthy Lifestyles

Cabbage and Potato Soup

½ lb.	lean ground pork	250 g
1	onion, diced	1
2	garlic cloves, minced	2
2 cups	packed, shredded cabbage	500 mL
2	tomatoes, diced	2
1	large potato, diced	1
5 cups	chicken stock*, page 43	1.25 L
1	bay leaf	1
1 tbsp.	chopped fresh dillweed OR	15 mL
	1 tsp. (5 mL) dried	
½ tsp.	paprika	2 mL
	salt and freshly ground pepper	
	to taste	

- In a soup pot or Dutch oven, over medium heat, brown ground pork.
- Blot up excess drippings with paper towel.
- Add onion and garlic; sauté for 5 minutes.
- Add cabbage; sauté for 2 minutes.
- Add tomatoes; sauté for 2 minutes.
- Add potato, chicken stock, bay leaf, dillweed and paprika.
- Simmer gently, uncovered, for 30 minutes.
- Season with salt and pepper to taste.

* If chicken stock is not available, substitute 4 tsp. (20 mL) of chicken bouillon granules and 5 cups (1.25 L) of boiling water.

Pictured on page 69.

Yield: 7 servings
Serving Size:
  1 cup (250 mL)
Preparation Time:
  20 minutes.

Nutritional Analysis
per serving

Calories	119
Protein	5.8 g
Carbohydrate	9.3 g
Fiber	1.7 g
Sugar	3 g
Fat	6.8 g
Cholesterol	12.7 mg
Saturated Fat	2.4 g
Mono Fat	2.2 g
Poly Fat	.7 g
Folate	22 Ug
Vitamin C	19 mg
Sodium	236 mg
Potassium	310 mg
Iron	1 mg
Calcium	25 mg

Turkey and Egg Drop Dumpling Soup

3 lbs.	turkey necks and backs*	1.5 kg
10 cups	water	2.5 L
1	onion, chopped	1
4	EACH celery stalks and carrots	4
1	bay leaf	1
¼ tsp.	crushed chili pepper	1 mL
2 tsp.	salt	10 mL
4	garlic cloves, crushed	4
1	leek, washed, sliced	1
2 tbsp.	chopped fresh dillweed OR	25 mL
	2 tsp. (10 mL) dried	
3	eggs	3
1 cup	all-purpose flour	250 mL
½ tsp.	salt	2 mL
	black pepper to taste	

- Rinse turkey parts. Place in a soup pot and add water. Over medium-high heat, bring to a simmer. Skim top frequently for about 15 minutes, until all scum has quit forming and is removed. Do not let soup come to a full boil.
- Add onion and 2 chopped celery stalks, 2 chopped carrots, bay leaf, crushed chili pepper and salt. Cover; gently simmer for 2½ hours.
- Strain; put stock in pot. Set bones aside to cool.
- Dice remaining carrots and celery. Add with garlic, leek and dillweed to stock. Simmer 30 minutes, or until vegetables are cooked.
- In a medium bowl, whisk together eggs, flour and salt. The dough should be stiff but still sticky.
- To make dumplings, fill a teaspoon about ⅓ full of dough, drawing it up the side of the bowl. Drop dumplings into the gently simmering soup. Cover; simmer for 10 minutes.
- Pick turkey meat from bones. Chop meat and add to soup. Season with pepper to taste.

* Use turkey or chicken carcasses also.

Yield: 12 servings
Freezes well
Serving Size:
  1 cup (250 mL)
Preparation Time:
  3 1/2 hours

Nutritional Analysis
per serving

Calories	221
Protein	24.5 g
Carbohydrate	13.9 g
Fiber	1.2 g
Sugar	3 g
Fat	7.4 g
Cholesterol	145 mg
Saturated Fat	2.3 g
Mono Fat	1.7 g
Poly Fat	1.9 g
Folate	24 Ug
Vitamin C	2 mg
Sodium	686 mg
Potassium	249 mg
Iron	3 mg
Calcium	55 mg

Smoked Cod Chowder

2 tbsp.	butter	25 mL
1 cup	chopped onion	250 mL
2	celery stalks, chopped	2
1½ cups	water	375 mL
1	medium potato, peeled, diced	1
1 cup	chopped fresh mixed vegetables OR frozen mixed vegetables	250 mL
8 oz.	boneless smoked cod, diced	225 g
13.5 oz.	can evaporated milk*	385 mL
¼ tsp.	salt	1 mL
	fresh ground pepper to taste	

- In a medium-sized saucepan, melt butter over medium heat.
- Add onion and celery. Sauté 5 minutes, stirring occasionally.
- Add water, potato and mixed vegetables.
- Bring to a boil, cover, reduce heat and simmer 30 minutes, or until vegetables are tender.
- Add cod, stir, cover and simmer 5 minutes.
- Add milk, heat without boiling.
- Season with salt and fresh ground pepper.

* Evaporated milk is used instead of light cream to add a creamy texture without added calories. If you prefer, substitute whole milk or light (cereal) cream.

Yield: 4 servings
Serving Size: 1 cup
(250 mL)
Preparation Time:
45 minutes

Nutritional Analysis
per serving

Calories	256
Protein	16.1 g
Carbohydrate	22.1 g
Fiber	2.9 g
Sugar	3 g
Fat	11.9 g
Cholesterol	73 mg
Saturated Fat	7.1 g
Mono Fat	3.5 g
Poly Fat	.6 g
Folate	28 Ug
Vitamin C	9 mg
Sodium	670 mg
Potassium	677 mg
Iron	1 mg
Calcium	251 mg

Nutrition Tips:

What is glycogen?
This is a form of carbohydrate that is stored in the muscle to be used primarily during short, high intensity exercise.

Autumn Soup

A medley of autumn vegetables blended with pears, coriander and nutmeg. A dash of cayenne adds zest.

5	parsnips, peeled, sliced in rounds	5
2	carrots, peeled, sliced in rounds	2
3	shallots, chopped	3
¼ cup	butter	50 mL
½ tsp.	ground coriander	2 mL
⅛ tsp.	ground nutmeg	0.5 mL
4	pears, cored, chopped	4
2 cups	zucchini, peeled, chopped	500 mL
4 cups	vegetable stock*, page 42	1 L
1 cup	whole milk	250 mL
dash	cayenne pepper	dash
¼ cup	chopped walnuts**	50 mL

- In a soup pot, over medium heat, sauté parsnips, carrots and shallots in butter for 5 minutes.
- Add coriander, nutmeg, pears, zucchini and stock. Stir well.
- Bring to a simmer and simmer 30 to 40 minutes, or until vegetables are soft. Remove from heat.
- Purée until smooth. Return to soup pot over medium heat.
- Add milk and cayenne pepper. Warm through. Do not boil.
- Garnish each bowl with 1 tsp. (5 mL) chopped walnuts.

Serve with banana bread, page 31. This is a great make-ahead meal. Freeze 1 or 2 serving portions for another meal.

* For convenience you can substitute 4 cups (1 L) of boiling water and 4 vegetable bouillon cubes.

** Garnish with chopped chives or green onion if you prefer.

Yield: 9 servings
Serving Size:
  1 cup (250 mL)
Preparation Time:
  1 hour

Nutritional Analysis
per serving

Calories	187
Protein	4 g
Carbohydrate	26 g
Fiber	4.8 g
Sugar	12.4 g
Fat	9.2 g
Cholesterol	18.2 mg
Saturated Fat	4.1 g
Mono Fat	2.4 g
Poly Fat	1.6 g
Folate	44 Ug
Vitamin C	12 mg
Sodium	524 mg
Potassium	470 mg
Iron	1 mg
Calcium	71 mg

Alphabet Tomato Soup*

Fresh tomato flavor makes an incredible soup in season. Make it all year round with hot house or canned tomatoes.

¼ cup	butter	50 mL
4 cups	chopped Roma tomatoes	1 L
¾ cup	chopped onion	175 mL
¾ cup	diced carrot	175 mL
1 tsp.	salt	5 mL
2 cups	water	500 mL
½, 5½ oz.	can tomato paste	½, 156 mL
½ cup	alphabet pasta	125 mL
1 tbsp.	granulated sugar	15 mL
1 tbsp.	all-purpose flour	15 mL
1 cup	cold water	250 mL

- In a large saucepan over medium to medium-low heat, melt butter.
- Add tomatoes, onions, carrot and salt. Sauté for 3 minutes.
- Add water and tomato paste and cover. Lower heat to medium-low and simmer for 30 minutes, until carrots are tender.
- Remove from heat; remove lid and cool for 5 minutes.
- Pour soup into a blender or food processor. Process until smooth. Pour back into saucepan.
- Cook pasta and drain.
- Reheat soup over medium heat. Add sugar.
- Mix flour with water. Stir well. Stir into soup. Cook and stir until soup comes to a boil.
- Reduce heat to low, cook for 5 minutes, stirring occasionally.
- Add cooked pasta and serve.

Use this **Basic Tomato Soup** in any recipes calling for tomato soup, make up a batch of soup without the pasta. Freeze in small batches. Makes about 7 cups (1.6 L) of Basic Tomato Soup.

Yield: 8 servings of Alphabet Tomato Soup

Serving Size: 1 cup (250 mL)
Preparation Time: 50 minutes

Nutritional Analysis

Tomato Soup with Pasta
1 cup (250 mL)

Calories	130
Protein	2.7 g
Carbohydrate	16.5 g
Fiber	2.2 g
Sugar	6.8 g
Fat	6.6 g
Cholesterol	16.4 mg
Saturated Fat	3.9 g
Mono Fat	1.8 g
Poly Fat	.4 g
Folate	21 Ug
Vitamin C	22 mg
Sodium	377 mg
Potassium	346 mg
Iron	1 mg
Calcium	18 mg

Basic Tomato Soup
½ cup (125 mL)

Calories	60
Protein	1.1 g
Carbohydrate	6.6 g
Fiber	1.2 g
Sugar	3.8 g
Fat	3.7 g
Cholesterol	9.3 mg
Saturated Fat	2.2 g
Mono Fat	1 g
Poly Fat	0 g
Folate	11 Ug
Vitamin C	12 mg
Sodium	215 mg
Potassium	191 mg
Iron	1 mg
Calcium	10 mg

Mushroom Soup

Savory mushroom soup is true comfort food.
This lower-fat version may also be used in any recipe
calling for mushroom soup or mushroom sauce.

1 cup	finely chopped onion	250 mL
¼ cup	butter	50 mL
4 cups	sliced mushrooms	1 L
1	garlic clove, minced	1
¼ cup	all-purpose flour	50 mL
1½ cups	water	375 mL
3 cups	1% milk	750 mL
2 tbsp.	cornstarch	25 mL
½ cup	cold water	125 mL
1 tbsp.	tomato paste	15 mL
1 tsp.	salt	5 mL
½ tsp.	black pepper	2 mL

- In a large saucepan over medium to medium-low heat, sauté onions in butter for 10 minutes, until they turn golden in color. Stir occasionally.
- Reduce heat to medium low, add mushrooms and garlic.
- Stir and cook for 5 minutes, stirring occasionally.
- Sprinkle with flour and stir well.
- Slowly add water, stirring constantly.
- Add milk and stir. Cook over medium heat until hot.
- In a small bowl, stir together cornstarch and water. Add to soup, stirring constantly until soup has come to a boil and is thickened.
- Reduce heat to low, add tomato paste, salt and pepper. Stir well until paste has dissolved.

Variations: Substitute equal quantities of chicken and beef stock for the milk. Omit cornstarch and water. For **Sherried Mushroom Soup**, add ¼ cup (50 mL) of sherry when sautéing mushrooms. Garnish with chopped green onions or chives.

Yield: 6 servings
Serving Size: 1 cup
 (250 mL)
Preparation Time:
 40 minutes

Nutritional Analysis
per serving

Calories	177
Protein	6.2 g
Carbohydrate	17.5 g
Fiber	1.3 g
Sugar	7.5 g
Fat	9.7 g
Cholesterol	26.7 mg
Saturated Fat	5.9 g
Mono Fat	2.7 g
Poly Fat	.5 g
Folate	23 Ug
Vitamin C	5 mg
Sodium	539 mg
Potassium	429 mg
Iron	1 mg
Calcium	164 mg

Basic Vegetable Stock*

Stock may include

> outer leaves of cabbage, lettuce or other greens; cauliflower and broccoli stalks; peels from washed carrots and parsnips OR whole carrots and parsnips; leeks, onions with skin on; garlic cloves; peppercorns

Small bouquet garni

2	sprigs parsley,	2
½	bay leaf	½
1	sprig fresh thyme OR ⅛ tsp. (0.5 mL) dried thyme – tie up into a small cheese-cloth bundle tied with string	1

- Chop vegetables coarsely and put into a soup pot.
- Cover with lightly salted water. Add a bouquet garni and 6 peppercorns.
- Bring to a boil; cover; reduce heat to a simmer. Simmer for 2 hours. Strain and cool.
- Stock can be frozen in small containers to be used when needed.

* These stocks were not analyzed because of the variables involved. Nutritional analysis is given in the various recipes using a commercial low-sodium stock which would have an analysis very similar to homemade stock.

Chicken Stock*

3½ lbs.	chicken backs and necks, rinsed	1.75 kg
16 cups	cold water	4 L
1	large onion, unpeeled, quartered	1
2	carrots, washed	2
2	celery stalks, leaves included, quartered	2
4	sprigs parsley	4
4	garlic cloves, halved	4
1 tsp.	salt	5 mL
10	whole black peppercorns	10
1	bay leaf	1
½ tsp.	curry powder	2 mL

- In a stock pot over medium-high heat, combine chicken and water.
- Bring to a simmer, skimming foam off the top and discarding.
- Reduce heat to maintain a very gentle simmer. Keep skimming until clear.
- Add onion, carrots, celery, parsley, garlic, salt, peppercorns, bay leaf and curry powder.
- Cover, leaving lid ajar. Simmer 3 hours.
- Discard bones and vegetables. Strain broth through a sieve.
- Let cool; refrigerate; remove fat from the top of the stock.

Note: Use whenever a recipe calls for chicken stock. Store in the refrigerator for up to 4 days or freeze in smaller containers to be used when needed.

* These stocks were not analyzed because of the variables involved. Nutritional analysis is given in the various recipes using a commercial low-sodium stock which would have an analysis very similar to homemade stock.

Basic Beef Stock*

4 lbs.	beef bones	2 kg
4 qts.	water	4 L
2	bay leaves	2
10	black peppercorns, lightly crushed	10
2	onions, unpeeled, quartered	2
2	carrots, chopped	2
2	celery stalks and leaves, chopped	2
	fresh parsley sprigs	

- In a stock pot or Dutch oven, combine beef bones, water, bay leaves, peppercorns.
- Bring to a boil; reduce heat and simmer for 1 hour. Add onions, carrots, celery and parsley. Simmer for 1 hour.
- Strain and cool.

* These stocks were not analyzed because of the variables involved. Nutritional analysis is given in the various recipes using a commercial low-sodium stock which would have an analysis very similar to homemade stock.

Ranch Dressing

A tangy salad dressing or use in recipes asking for ranch dressing. To use as a dip, use only ⅓ cup (75 mL) buttermilk.

1 cup	buttermilk	250 mL
⅓ cup	light mayonnaise	75 mL
1	garlic clove, crushed	1
1 tbsp.	chopped fresh parsley OR 1 tsp. (5 mL) dried	15 mL
¼ tsp.	EACH dried dillweed, crushed basil, crushed oregano	1 mL
¼ tsp.	dry mustard	1 mL
⅛ tsp.	freshly ground pepper	0.5 mL

- In a bowl, whisk together all ingredients. Store in a sealed container.

Yield: 1⅓ cups (325 mL)
Serving Size: 2 tbsp. (30 mL)
Preparation Time: 10 minutes

Nutritional Analysis
per serving

Calories	33
Protein	.5 g
Carbohydrate	2.1 g
Fiber	.8 g
Sugar	1.2 g
Fat	2.7 g
Cholesterol	0 mg
Saturated Fat	.5 g
Mono Fat	.3 g
Poly Fat	.8 g
Folate	12 Ug
Vitamin C	5 mg
Sodium	65 mg
Potassium	57 mg
Iron	0 mg
Calcium	10 mg

Baby Greens with Fresh Lemon Dressing

¼ lb.	mixed baby greens OR mesclun*	125 g
⅓, 4.2 oz.	container pea sprouts OR other sprouts	⅓, 120 g
2 tbsp.	canola oil	25 mL
2 tbsp.	fresh lemon juice	25 mL
2 tsp.	granulated sugar	10 mL
¼ tsp.	seasoning salt	1 mL
1 tbsp.	shelled, toasted sunflower seeds	15 mL

- In a salad bowl, toss together baby greens and sprouts.
- In a small bowl, whisk together oil, lemon juice, sugar and salt until creamy.
- Drizzle the dressing over the greens and toss lightly. Sprinkle with sunflower seeds. Serve salad immediately.

* Mixed baby greens or mesclun can be purchased loose or packaged in the produce department. Remaining sprouts can be used in a sandwich.

Pictured on page 51.

Pictured on page 51.

Yield: 4 servings

Serving Size: 1 cup
(250 mL)
Preparation Time:
5 minutes

Nutritional Analysis

per serving

Calories	95
Protein	1.3 g
Carbohydrate	5.4 g
Fiber	1 g
Sugar	3.1 g
Fat	8.3 g
Cholesterol	0 mg
Saturated Fat	.6 g
Mono Fat	4.7 g
Poly Fat	2.8 g
Folate	35 Ug
Vitamin C	13 mg
Sodium	120 mg
Potassium	133 mg
Iron	1 mg
Calcium	35 mg

Nutrition Tips:

Vegetarians must be careful in selecting foods in order to obtain a balanced mixture of amino acids. Other nutrients to watch for are Vitamin B12, Calcium, Iron, Zinc.

Back-To-Basics Salad

This dressing tastes like the wonderful, old-fashioned sour milk/sour cream dressing made on farms years ago.

3 cups	chopped lettuce	750 mL
1	tomato, diced	1
½ cup	diced cucumber	125 mL
4	large radishes, sliced	4
1	celery stalk, sliced	1
1	green onion, sliced	1

Tangy Mayonnaise Dressing

¼ cup	mayonnaise	50 mL
2 tbsp.	2% milk	25 mL
1 tsp.	white vinegar	5 mL
1 tsp.	granulated sugar	5 mL
	dash of salt	
	black pepper to taste	

- In a salad bowl, toss together lettuce, tomato, cucumber, radish, celery and green onion.
- In a small bowl, mix together mayonnaise, milk, vinegar, sugar, salt and pepper. Drizzle over salad. Toss lightly to coat.

Nutrition Tips:

The precompetition meal should be easily digestible, high in complex carbohydrate, low in protein and in fat, and should be consumed 3 to 4 hours prior to competition.

Goals of the precompetition meal:
- allow the stomach to be empty at the start of competition.
- avoid stomach cramps
- help avoid the sensation of hunger, light-headedness, fatigue.
- provide adequate fuel supplies, mostly carbohydrate, in blood and muscle.
- provide adequate hydration

Yield: 5 servings
Serving Size: 1 cup
(250 mL)
Preparation Time:
11 minutes

Nutritional Analysis
per serving

Calories	99
Protein	.9 g
Carbohydrate	3.8 g
Fiber	1 g
Sugar	2.8 g
Fat	9.1 g
Cholesterol	8.5 mg
Saturated Fat	1.7 g
Mono Fat	1 g
Poly Fat	5.2 g
Folate	28 Ug
Vitamin C	8 mg
Sodium	76 mg
Potassium	166 mg
Iron	0 mg
Calcium	21 mg

Tabbouleh

Tabbouleh (or Tabouli) is a very refreshing salad. It literally bursts with flavor.

1 cup	bulgur, preferably fine	250 mL
1	medium onion, minced	1
1	medium tomato, finely diced	1
1 cup	minced parsley	250 mL
½ cup	minced fresh mint OR ¼ cup (50 mL) crushed dried mint	125 mL
¼ cup	fresh lemon juice	50 mL
¼ cup	olive oil	50 mL
½ tsp.	salt	2 mL
¼ tsp.	black pepper	1 mL

- Mix bulgur with 2 cups (500 mL) of cold water. Let stand for 30 minutes at room temperature. Drain well in a sieve.
- In a bowl, combine bulgur with onion. Stir well.
- Add tomato, parsley and mint. Stir.
- In a small bowl, combine lemon juice, olive oil, salt and pepper. Pour over bulgur mixture, mixing well.
- Refrigerate for at least 1 hour.

Serve with Marinated Broiled Lamb Chops, page 165, or steak or with toasted pita as a lunch dish.

Variation: Some Tabbouleh versions use up to 3 cups (750 mL) of parsley to ⅓ cup (75 mL) of dry bulgur. Red onion or green onion may be substituted for white onions. 1 to 2 minced garlic cloves may also be added to the salad.

Yield: 9 servings

Serving Size: ½ cup (125 mL)
Preparation Time: 45 minutes

Nutritional Analysis

per serving

Calories	83
Protein	1.1 g
Carbohydrate	6.7 g
Fiber	1.6 g
Sugar	.9 g
Fat	6.2 g
Cholesterol	0 mg
Saturated Fat	.8 g
Mono Fat	4.5 g
Poly Fat	.6 g
Folate	22 Ug
Vitamin C	16 mg
Sodium	136 mg
Potassium	117 mg
Iron	1 mg
Calcium	20 mg

Romaine and Pear Salad with Blue Cheese Dressing

| 1 head | romaine lettuce, washed, trimmed and torn into bite-size pieces | 1 head |

Blue Cheese Dressing

¼ cup	light mayonnaise	50 mL
¼ cup	1% milk	50 mL
¼ cup	crumbled blue cheese	50 mL
1 tsp.	lemon juice	5 mL
1 tsp.	balsamic vinegar black pepper to taste	5 mL
1	red pear (or any type of pear), thinly sliced	1
2 tbsp.	chopped walnuts	25 mL

- Prepare lettuce.
- In a small bowl, combine mayonnaise, milk, 2 tbsp. (25 mL) blue cheese, lemon juice and balsamic vinegar. Stir well. Add pepper to taste.
- In a salad bowl, toss romaine with dressing.
- Arrange red pear slices over the salad. Sprinkle with the remaining blue cheese and walnuts. Serve.

Nutrition Tips:

Did you know that regular physical training increases the ability of muscles to store and use carbohydrate for energy production?

Low levels of blood glucose or muscle glycogen may be contributing factors in the early onset of fatigue in prolonged exercise.

Yield:
4 large salads
Serving Size: 2 cups (500 mL)
Preparation Time: 15 minutes

Nutritional Analysis
per serving

Calories	129
Protein	5 g
Carbohydrate	11 g
Fiber	2.9 g
Sugar	6.8 g
Fat	7.7 g
Cholesterol	.6 mg
Saturated Fat	1.3 g
Mono Fat	1.2 g
Poly Fat	3 g
Folate	102 Ug
Vitamin C	19 mg
Sodium	174 mg
Potassium	312 mg
Iron	1 mg
Calcium	113 mg

Yield: 4 servings
Serving Size: ½ cup
  (125 mL)
Preparation Time:
  15 minutes

Nutritional Analysis
per serving

Calories	42
Protein	3.5 g
Carbohydrate	6.9 g
Fiber	.6 g
Sugar	4.9 g
Fat	.2 g
Cholesterol	1.1 mg
Saturated Fat	.1 g
Mono Fat	0 g
Poly Fat	0 g
Folate	16 Ug
Vitamin C	5 mg
Sodium	45 mg
Potassium	259 mg
Iron	0 mg
Calcium	115 mg

Yield: 6 servings
Serving Size: ½ cup
  (125 mL)
Preparation Time:
  12 minutes.

Nutritional Analysis
per serving

Calories	139
Protein	3 g
Carbohydrate	13.3 g
Fiber	1.3 g
Sugar	10.9 g
Fat	8.6 g
Cholesterol	10.1 mg
Saturated Fat	3 g
Mono Fat	1.6 g
Poly Fat	1.9 g
Folate	10 Ug
Vitamin C	5 mg
Sodium	175 mg
Potassium	149 mg
Iron	0 mg
Calcium	83 mg

Cool Cucumber Salad

Famous throughout the middle east, this refreshing salad is known as Tzatziki in Greece and as Khiar bi Laban (yogurt) in Lebanon. Instead of dillweed, chopped fresh mint is used for garnish in the Lebanese version.

1 cup	no-fat plain yogurt	250 mL
1	garlic clove, crushed	1
1 tsp.	fresh lemon juice	5 mL
1 tbsp.	chopped fresh dillweed	15 mL
	salt and black pepper to taste	
1	English cucumber, thinly sliced	1

- In a bowl, blend yogurt, garlic, lemon juice, dillweed, salt and pepper. Cover and chill until ready to serve.
- In a serving bowl, place thinly sliced cucumber. Gently toss with yogurt dressing. Serve immediately.

Apple, Grape and Cheddar Salad

⅓ cup	light mayonnaise	75 mL
2 tbsp.	1% milk	25 mL
2 tsp.	lemon juice	10 mL
2 tsp.	granulated sugar	10 mL
2	apples, cored, diced	2
½ cup	diced celery	125 mL
½ cup	halved red or green seedless grapes	125 mL
½ cup	coarsely shredded Cheddar cheese	125 mL
1 tbsp.	raw sunflower seeds	15 mL

- In a serving bowl mix mayonnaise, milk, lemon juice and sugar.
- Add apples; toss to coat. Add celery, grapes and cheese; toss. Sprinkle with sunflower seeds.

Strawberry Salad with
Poppy Seed Honey Yogurt Dressing

| 1 | large (or 2 small) butter lettuce, washed, dried | 1 |
| 2 cups | sliced fresh strawberries | 500 mL |

Poppy Seed Honey Yogurt Dressing

½ cup	no-fat strawberry yogurt	125 mL
1 tbsp.	raspberry vinegar	15 mL
2 tsp.	honey	10 mL
1½ tsp.	poppy seeds	7 mL
1½ tsp.	toasted sesame seeds	7 mL
⅛ tsp.	ground ginger	0.5 mL

- Divide lettuce among 4 salad plates, tearing the larger leaves.
- Arrange ½ cup (125 mL) sliced strawberries on lettuce.
- In a small bowl, mix together yogurt, vinegar, honey, poppy seeds, sesame seeds and ginger.
- Drizzle the dressing over the salads, about 2 tbsp. (25 mL) each.

Note: Salad plates and dressing may be made up and kept separate, covered with plastic wrap, in refrigerator for about 1 hour.

Lunches, At Home & Portable

Baby Greens with
Fresh Lemon Dressing, page 45

Yield: 4 servings
Serving Size:
  Approximately 2 cups
  (500 mL)
Preparation Time:
  15 minutes

Nutritional Analysis
per serving

Calories	135
Protein	3.3 g
Carbohydrate	31.7 g
Fiber	2.9 g
Sugar	4.3 g
Fat	1.2 g
Cholesterol	.6 mg
Saturated Fat	.1 g
Mono Fat	.1 g
Poly Fat	.4 g
Folate	45 Ug
Vitamin C	53 mg
Sodium	25 mg
Potassium	255 mg
Iron	1 mg
Calcium	71 mg

Tomato and Mushroom Salad

Yield:

6 servings

Serving Size: ½ cup
(125 mL)
Preparation Time:
12 minutes

Balsamic Basil Dressing

¼ cup	olive oil	50 mL
2 tbsp.	balsamic vinegar	25 mL
2 tbsp.	chopped fresh basil	25 mL
2 tsp.	sugar	10 mL
½ tsp.	curry powder	2 tsp.
1	garlic clove, crushed	1
4	medium tomatoes, thickly sliced	4
1 cup	sliced mushrooms	250 mL
2	green onions, sliced	2
½ cup	croûtons*	125 mL

- In a jar with a tight fitting lid, combine oil, vinegar, basil, sugar, curry powder and garlic. Shake well.
- On a serving plate, arrange tomato slices overlapping each other. Arrange mushrooms on top. Sprinkle with onions. Drizzle dressing over. Sprinkle with croûtons.

Pictured on page 159.

* **Homemade Croûtons** are delicious and easy to prepare. They can be varied with garlic, herbs, lemon pepper, seasoning salt, olive or flavored oils and Parmesan cheese. Sprinkle cubes of bread with oil, herbs, etc. Bake at 300°F (150°C), stirring occasionally until golden brown, or sauté until browned. To make **Low-Fat Croûtons** spray bread cubes with nonstick spray and toss with herbs, garlic, low-fat Parmesan cheese, etc., and bake until browned. Stir occasionally.

Nutritional Analysis
per serving

Calories	126
Protein	1.5 g
Carbohydrate	10 g
Fiber	1.5 g
Sugar	5.3 g
Fat	9.6 g
Cholesterol	0 mg
Saturated Fat	1.3 g
Mono Fat	6.8 g
Poly Fat	.9 g
Folate	17 Ug
Vitamin C	17 mg
Sodium	103 mg
Potassium	282 mg
Iron	1 mg
Calcium	33 mg

Broccoli Corn Salad

1½ cups	broccoli florets, cut into bite-sized pieces	375 mL
1 cup	frozen OR canned kernel corn	250 mL
1	carrot, thinly sliced	1
10	cherry tomatoes, halved	10

Garlic Vinegar Dressing

1 tbsp.	canola oil	15 mL
2 tbsp.	white vinegar	25 mL
1 tbsp.	granulated sugar	15 mL
1	garlic clove, finely minced	1
¼ tsp.	paprika	1 mL
¼ tsp.	celery seed	1 mL
½ tsp.	seasoning salt	2 mL
	black pepper to taste	

- In a salad bowl, combine broccoli, corn, carrot slices, and cherry tomatoes.
- In a small bowl, stir together oil, vinegar, sugar, garlic, paprika, celery seed, seasoning salt and pepper until sugar is dissolved.
- Pour the dressing over the salad. Toss. Refrigerate for 15 minutes. Toss again and serve.

Yield: 4 servings
Serving size: 1 cup (250 mL)
Preparation time: 15 minutes

Nutrition Tips:

What happens to protein in the body?

Proteins are broken down into amino acids and absorbed into the bloodstream. Body cells pick up amino acids from the blood and use only what is necessary to fulfill their needs. Cells can't store excess amino acids, therefore the nitrogen is excreted in the urine and the energy portion of the amino acid is converted to carbohydrate or fat. Therefore, protein supplements and megadosing are ineffective ways of improving performance.

Nutritional Analysis
per serving

Calories	111
Protein	3 g
Carbohydrate	19 g
Fiber	3 g
Sugar	7.3 g
Fat	4.2 g
Cholesterol	0 mg
Saturated Fat	.3 g
Mono Fat	2.4 g
Poly Fat	1.3 g
Folate	49 Ug
Vitamin C	44 mg
Sodium	212 mg
Potassium	391 mg
Iron	1 mg
Calcium	28 mg

Broiled Vegetable

2	medium red potatoes	
1	red pepper, seeded, quartered	
1	zucchini, cut into ¼" (6 mm) diagonal slices	
4	green onions, sliced into 2" (5 cm) lengths	4
2	¼" (6 mm) slices of red onion	2
2	Roma tomatoes, halved	2
2	large Portobello mushrooms OR 8 regular white mushrooms*	2
3 tbsp.	olive oil	45 mL
	freshly ground pepper	
2 tbsp.	balsamic vinegar	25 mL
1	garlic clove, mashed	1
2 tbsp.	chopped fresh basil	25 mL
½ tsp.	salt	2 mL

- Preheat broiler.
- Parboil the potatoes in the microwave on High for 4 to 5 minutes. Slice into ¼" (6 mm) slices.
- In a large bowl, toss potato slices, red pepper, zucchini, green onion, red onion, tomatoes and mushrooms with 1 tbsp. (15 mL) olive oil and the pepper.
- Lay vegetables on a broiling rack.
- Broil 6" (15 cm) from heat for 10 minutes each side.
- In a salad bowl, combine 2 tbsp. (25 mL) olive oil, balsamic vinegar, garlic, basil and salt.
- Toss broiled vegetables in the dressing.
- Cool for 10 to 15 minutes.

Serve with sourdough bread.

* Don't be intimidated by exotically named mushrooms, white or button mushrooms, which are good all-purpose mushrooms, are also called Champignon de Paris.

Yield: 4 servings
Serving Size: 1 cup (250 mL)
Preparation Time: 15 minutes

Nutritional Analysis
per serving

Calories	236
Protein	4.4 g
Carbohydrate	33.2 g
Fiber	4.7 g
Sugar	4.4 g
Fat	10.6 g
Cholesterol	0 mg
Saturated Fat	1.4 g
Mono Fat	7.5 g
Poly Fat	1 g
Folate	38 Ug
Vitamin C	73 mg
Sodium	309 mg
Potassium	718 mg
Iron	2 mg
Calcium	38 mg

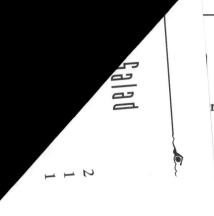

Ranch Dressing

	rtellini	350 g
		250 mL
		125 mL
		250 mL
	oled, chopped	2
		1
		1
2	green onions, sliced	2
	salt and pepper to taste	
¾ cup	Ranch Dressing*, page 44	175 mL

- Cook tortellini as per package directions. Drain and rinse under cold water. Drain well.
- Rinse peas under cold water. Drain.
- In a large salad bowl, combine red pepper, ham, eggs, carrot, celery and green onions.
- Add tortellini, peas, salt and pepper. Stir.
- Pour ½ cup (125 mL) ranch dressing over. Mix well.
- Cover and chill for 1 hour.
- Just before serving, stir in ¼ cup (50 mL) Ranch Dressing.

* Use homemade Ranch Dressing, page 44, or for convenience try a commercial ranch-style dressing.

Yield: 8 servings
Serving Size: 1 cup (250 mL)
Preparation Time: 30 minutes

Nutritional Analysis
per serving

Calories	224
Protein	10.2 g
Carbohydrate	17.6 g
Fiber	2.2 g
Sugar	3.1 g
Fat	12.9 g
Cholesterol	73.9 mg
Saturated Fat	2.8 g
Mono Fat	2.6 g
Poly Fat	4.3 g
Folate	24 Ug
Vitamin C	12 mg
Sodium	475 mg
Potassium	115 mg
Iron	1 mg
Calcium	74 mg

Chef's Salad To Go

2 cups	lightly packed, chopped lettuce	500 mL
2 oz.	sliced lean cooked ham, julienned	60 g
2 oz.	sliced turkey OR chicken	60 g
2 oz.	Swiss cheese, julienned	60 g
1	carrot, thinly sliced diagonally	1
16	cucumber slices	16
1	medium tomato, cut into 8 wedges	1
2	hard-boiled eggs, quartered lengthwise	2
2 tbsp.	salad dressing (your favorite)	25 mL
	salt and black pepper to taste	

- For a portable lunch, in each of 2 plastic, sealable luncheon containers, arrange half of the chopped lettuce, ham, turkey or chicken and cheese in a spoke fashion on the lettuce.
- Sprinkle each with half of the carrot slices.
- Arrange cucumber slices around the outside of the lettuce, tucking slices partway under the lettuce.
- Place 4 tomato wedges vertically around the salad.
- Place quartered egg vertically between tomato wedges.
- Top with your favorite dressing or include dressing in a small separate container.
- Salad will keep, covered, in refrigerator for up to 8 hours.
- Salt and pepper just before serving.

Serve with bread sticks.

Variations: For a make-ahead, at-home lunch, arrange salad on plates, cover with plastic wrap and refrigerate. Use leftover ham, turkey or chicken if you wish.

Yield: 2 servings

Serving Size: 2½ cups (625 mL)

Preparation time: 15 minutes

Nutritional Analysis
per serving

Calories	368
Protein	26.1 g
Carbohydrate	15.1 g
Fiber	3.4 g
Sugar	6.7 g
Fat	22.8 g
Cholesterol	257.1 mg
Saturated Fat	8.3 g
Mono Fat	6.5 g
Poly Fat	5.5 g
Folate	121 Ug
Vitamin C	31 mg
Sodium	779 mg
Potassium	692 mg
Iron	2 mg
Calcium	342 mg

Turkey Sub with Honey Mustard Mayo

Honey Mustard Mayo

2 tbsp.	light mayonnaise	25 mL
1 tbsp.	honey	15 mL
4 tsp.	dijon mustard	20 mL
1, 6"	submarine OR hoagie bun	1, 15 cm
2 tbsp.	honey mustard mayo	25 mL
1 oz.	sliced turkey breast	30 g
1 oz.	sliced lean turkey kielbasa OR salami	30 g
1 oz.	thinly sliced smoked Gruyère cheese (OR any cheese)	30 g
⅛"	slice of red onion, separated into rings	4 mm
⅓ cup	loosely packed shredded lettuce	75 mL
2 tsp.	light Italian dressing	10 mL
4, ⅛"	slices of tomato	4, 4 mm
	salt and black pepper to taste	
	alfalfa sprouts	

- To prepare Honey Mustard Mayo, in a small bowl combine the mayonnaise, honey and mustard until blended.
- To prepare sub, open submarine bun and lay flat.
- Spread 1 tbsp. (15 mL) Honey Mustard Mayo on each half.
- On the bottom bun, lay the turkey breast, then turkey kielbasa.
- Add in layers, the cheese, onion and lettuce.
- Drizzle Italian dressing over.
- Top with tomato, salt and pepper.
- Pinch a tuft of sprouts, loosen strands, and spread sprouts on top of tomato.
- Cover with top half of bun and cut in half crosswise.

Yield: 1 serving
Serving Size: 1 sub
Preparation Time:
  10 minutes

Nutritional Analysis
per serving

Calories	888
Protein	33.5 g
Carbohydrate	93.5 g
Fiber	5.2 g
Sugar	23.1 g
Fat	42.9 g
Cholesterol	78 mg
Saturated Fat	11.8 g
Mono Fat	11.8 g
Poly Fat	6.1 g
Folate	40 Ug
Vitamin C	16 mg
Sodium	2109 mg
Potassium	491 mg
Iron	5 mg
Calcium	420 mg

Shrimp, Tomato and Lettuce Wraps

4, 10"	flour tortillas	4, 25 cm
½ cup	light spreadable cream cheese	125 mL
½ cup	tomato-based seafood sauce	125 mL
2	green onions, thinly sliced	2
1⅓ cups	shredded lettuce	325 mL
2	small tomatoes, diced	2
½ cup	thinly sliced celery	125 mL
4 oz.	can small shrimp, rinsed and drained	113 g

- For each wrap, lay out a tortilla.
- Spread with 2 tbsp. (25 mL) cream cheese then 2 tbsp. (25 mL) seafood sauce. Sprinkle a quarter of the green onion over each.
- Lay ⅓ cup (75 mL) lettuce down the center. Sprinkle ½ a diced tomato, 2 tbsp. (25 mL) celery and ¼ of the shrimp on top of the lettuce.
- Fold the bottom of the tortilla up ¼ of the way. Wrap sides snugly over one other, leaving the top open.

Note: Wrap in paper towel then waxed paper if packing for a portable lunch.

Variations: Tuna may be substituted for shrimp.

Yield: 4 servings
Serving Size: 1 wrap
Preparation Time:
  16 minutes

Nutritional Analysis
per serving

Calories	252
Protein	13 g
Carbohydrate	31.6 g
Fiber	2.9 g
Sugar	8.8 g
Fat	7.7 g
Cholesterol	15 mg
Saturated Fat	3.9 g
Mono Fat	1 g
Poly Fat	1.1 g
Folate	46 Ug
Vitamin C	17 mg
Sodium	873 mg
Potassium	385 mg
Iron	2 mg
Calcium	123 mg

Nutrition Tips:

If you are taking a supplement, here is something to try. Drop a tablet in some vinegar, gently stir. If the tablet isn't dissolved in 20 to 30 minutes, then it wouldn't get digested by the stomach acids either. Therefore, it would be of little nutritional value to you.

Bean Burritos

Tortillas

1 cup	all-purpose flour	250 mL
½ cup	cornmeal	125 mL
¼ tsp.	salt	1 mL
1⅔ cups	cold water	400 mL
	canola oil	
14 oz.	can refried beans	398 mL
⅓ cup	taco sauce	75 mL
½ cup	chopped onion	125 mL

- In a medium bowl, combine flour, cornmeal, salt and water. Beat until consistency is smooth.
- Preheat a griddle or heavy frying pan over medium heat. Wipe griddle surface with oil.
- Using a ⅓ cup (75 mL) measure, scoop batter; pour onto griddle; rotate to make a round tortilla.
- Cook 1 minute, until edges look dry. Flip and cook 20 seconds. Wipe surface of griddle with oil as needed to keep tortillas from sticking.
- Keep tortillas warm in oven, until you are finished cooking all tortillas, or let cool.
- Heat refried beans in a microwave-safe bowl on High for 2 minutes, or until hot.
- Lay a tortilla on a flat surface. Scoop ¼ cup (50 mL) beans down center of tortilla, add 2 tsp. (10 mL) taco sauce, 1 tbsp. (15 mL) onion.
- Starting at the bottom of the beans, fold tortilla up about 1" (2.5 cm). Fold in 1 side then wrap the other side snugly over.
- To reheat in microwave, lay tortilla on paper towel and microwave on High for 10-20 seconds.

Variations: Fry ground beef with taco seasoning. Top tortilla with meat mixture and grated Cheddar. Fold as above. Spread tortilla with sour cream or salsa; top with chopped lettuce, tomato, onion and grated Cheddar. Fold. Leftover tortillas are great spread with strawberry jam and rolled up.

Yield: 8 servings (8 burritos)
Serving Size: 1 burrito
Preparation time: 22 minutes

Nutritional Analysis
per serving

Calories	158
Protein	5.3 g
Carbohydrate	27.9 g
Fiber	3.9 g
Sugar	.5 g
Fat	2.9 g
Cholesterol	4 mg
Saturated Fat	0 g
Mono Fat	0 g
Poly Fat	.1 g
Folate	16 Ug
Vitamin C	7 mg
Sodium	265 mg
Potassium	206 mg
Iron	2 mg
Calcium	25 mg

Mushroom Burgers

1 cup	cooked, cooled brown rice	250 mL
2 cups	shredded mushrooms	500 mL
½ cup	shredded carrot	125 mL
⅓ cup	shredded onion	75 mL
1	egg, beaten	1
2	garlic cloves, crushed	2
2 tbsp.	raw sunflower seeds	25 mL
½ cup	quick-cooking oatmeal	125 mL
⅓ cup	natural bran	75 mL
2 tbsp.	soy sauce	25 mL
½ tsp.	seasoning salt	2 mL
¼ tsp.	black pepper	1 mL
¼ tsp.	crushed thyme	1 mL
2 tbsp.	Parmesan cheese	25 mL
½ cup	shredded mozzarella cheese	125 mL
1 cup	pancake OR biscuit mix	250 mL
	olive oil	

- In a large bowl, combine brown rice, mushrooms, carrot, onion, egg and garlic.
- Add sunflower seeds, oatmeal, bran, soy sauce, seasoning salt, pepper, thyme, Parmesan cheese and mozzarella. Stir well.
- Add pancake mix to just thicken. It will thicken more as it stands for a few minutes.
- Heat 1 tsp. (5 mL) olive oil in a large nonstick frying pan.
- Using a ¼ cup (50 mL) measure, scoop mushroom mixture into the frying pan, flatten and shape to a ½" (1 cm) thick, 3" (8 cm) round with a pancake turner. Cook for 2½ minutes, until browned. Flip over and cook another 2 minutes.
- Serve as a regular hamburger with tomato, lettuce, mustard, ketchup, etc. or remove burgers to a cooling rack, cool, package in an airtight bag or container. Refrigerate or freeze. To reheat, place burgers on a paper towel and microwave on Low for 1½ minutes.

Yield: 6 servings
Serving Size: 2 patties
Preparation Time:
  30 minutes

Nutritional Analysis
per serving

Calories	253
Protein	9.7 g
Carbohydrate	34.1 g
Fiber	4.1 g
Sugar	5 g
Fat	9.8 g
Cholesterol	41.9 mg
Saturated Fat	2.8 g
Mono Fat	3.3 g
Poly Fat	3 g
Folate	42 Ug
Vitamin C	3 mg
Sodium	850 mg
Potassium	316 mg
Iron	3 mg
Calcium	150 mg

Denver Sandwich

A flavor favorite for generations, this sandwich is a classic.

3	strips of bacon, diced	3
½ tsp.	canola oil	2 mL
2 tbsp.	diced onion	25 mL
¼	green pepper, diced	¼
4	mushrooms, sliced	4
2	eggs	2
2 tbsp.	water	25 mL
1 tsp.	Worcestershire sauce	5 mL
4	slices flax bread (OR any bread), toasted	4
4	slices tomato	4
	salt and pepper to taste	

- In a medium-sized, nonstick frying pan, over medium heat, sauté bacon for 5 minutes. Drain off fat.
- Add the oil, onion and the green pepper. Cook for 2 minutes, stirring occasionally.
- Add mushrooms, cook for 1½ minutes. Reduce heat to medium-low.
- In a small bowl, whisk eggs, water and Worcestershire until foamy.
- Quickly pour eggs into the frying pan. Stir until they start to set.
- Lift edges all around to let egg run under to cook.
- When nicely browned, flip over; cook the other side for 2 minutes, or until browned.
- Cut omelet in half, place each half on a slice of toast. Top each with 2 slices of tomato, salt and pepper and the remaining toast slices. Cut sandwiches in half to serve.

Yield: 2 servings
Serving Size: 1 sandwich
Preparation Time: 10 minutes

Nutritional Analysis
per serving

Calories	296
Protein	15.8 g
Carbohydrate	34.5 g
Fiber	4.8 g
Sugar	1.5 g
Fat	12 g
Cholesterol	220 mg
Saturated Fat	3.3 g
Mono Fat	4.9 g
Poly Fat	1.6 g
Folate	95 Ug
Vitamin C	23 mg
Sodium	383 mg
Potassium	261 mg
Iron	2 mg
Calcium	163 mg

Broiled Tuna and Egg Bagel

3	hard-boiled eggs, shelled	3
6.5 oz.	can flaked tuna in water	184 g
½ cup	grated Cheddar cheese	125 mL
¼ cup	light mayonnaise	50 mL
2 tbsp.	thinly sliced green onion	25 mL
12	stuffed olives, sliced	12
4	whole-wheat bagels (½ bagel per serving)	4

- In a medium bowl, mash eggs with a fork or chop coarsely.
- Add tuna; mix well, breaking up large flakes.
- Add cheese, mayonnaise, onions and olives, mix well.
- Spread ¼ cup (50 mL) of filling on each bagel half.
- Preheat broiler, broil bagels 6" (15 cm) from heat for 5 minutes, or until tops are browned and puffed.

Serve with soup or salad.

Variations: Top with additional cheese before broiling, if you wish. Tuna egg filling may also be used cold as a spread for rice cakes or crackers or as a filling for celery sticks.

Pictured on page 69.

Yield: 8 servings
Serving Size: ¼ cup (50 mL) of filling and ½ bagel each
Preparation Time: 15 minutes

Nutritional Analysis
per serving

Calories	202
Protein	13.4 g
Carbohydrate	25.3 g
Fiber	4 g
Sugar	.6 g
Fat	9 g
Cholesterol	98 mg
Saturated Fat	2.6 g
Mono Fat	2.2 g
Poly Fat	1 g
Folate	100 Ug
Vitamin C	0 mg
Sodium	420 mg
Potassium	37 mg
Iron	2 mg
Calcium	286 mg

Hot Dog Pizza

Hot dogs and pizza combined – a great lunch for kids.

1	whole-wheat hot dog bun, cut in half lengthwise	1
2 tbsp.	Basic Tomato Sauce, page 128	25 mL
3 tbsp.	1% cottage cheese	45 mL
2 tbsp.	grated Cheddar cheese	25 mL
1	chicken wiener, cut into ¼" (6 mm) semicircles OR 2 mushrooms sliced OR pineapple tidbits	1
¼ tsp.	Italian seasoning	1 mL

- Preheat broiler.
- Lay opened hot dog bun on a baking sheet.
- Spread 1 tbsp. (15 mL) of tomato sauce on each half.
- In a small bowl, combine cottage cheese with Cheddar.
- Divide cheese mixture between buns; spread out.
- Top with chicken wiener slices, mushrooms or pineapple tidbits.
- Sprinkle with Italian seasoning.
- Broil 4" (10 cm) from heat for 2 to 2½ minutes.
- Cool for 1 to 2 minutes. Cut each bun in half crosswise.

Serve with carrot and cucumber sticks.

Yield: 2 servings
Serving Size:
  1 bun half
Preparation Time:
  8 minutes

Nutritional Analysis
per serving

Calories	140
Protein	9.5 g
Carbohydrate	15.5 g
Fiber	1.4 g
Sugar	2.7 g
Fat	4.6 g
Cholesterol	20.4 mg
Saturated Fat	1.9 g
Mono Fat	1.2 g
Poly Fat	1.2 g
Folate	12 Ug
Vitamin C	1 mg
Sodium	631 mg
Potassium	141 mg
Iron	1 mg
Calcium	81 mg

Ham and Pineapple Pita Pizza

2, 6"	pitas	2, 15 cm
1 cup	Béchamel Sauce, page 134	250 mL
4 tsp.	Parmesan cheese	20 mL
4 oz.	sliced Black Forest ham, chopped	118 g
4	mushrooms, thinly sliced	4
½, 8 oz.	can pineapple, drained	½, 227 mL
½ cup	shredded Cheddar cheese	125 mL

Turkey and Mushroom Pita Pizza

2, 6"	pitas	6, 15 cm
4 tbsp.	thick barbecue sauce OR Basic Tomato Sauce, page 128	50 mL
4 oz.	sliced cooked turkey meat, chopped	118 g
4	mushrooms, sliced	4
½ cup	shredded mozzarella cheese	125 mL

- Preheat oven to 375°F (190°C).
- Lay out pitas on a baking sheet.
- Top 2 of the pitas with ½ cup (125 mL) béchamel sauce.
- Sprinkle 2 tsp. (10 mL) Parmesan over each.
- Add a layer of ham, mushrooms and pineapple.
- Divide the Cheddar between the 2 pizzas.
- On the other 2 pizzas, spread 2 tbsp. (25 mL) barbecue or basic tomato sauce on each.
- Top with turkey, mushrooms, pineapple and mozzarella.
- Bake pizzas for 15 to 20 minutes on the middle oven rack.
- Cut each pizza into 4.

Yield: 8 servings (16 slices)

Serving Size: 2 wedges
Preparation Time: 15 minutes

Nutritional Analysis

per serving

Ham Pizza

Calories	122
Protein	7.1 g
Carbohydrate	12.5 g
Fiber	.5 g
Sugar	3.2 g
Fat	4.9 g
Cholesterol	15.3 mg
Saturated Fat	2.2 g
Mono Fat	1.8 g
Poly Fat	.5 g
Folate	8 Ug
Vitamin C	1 mg
Sodium	375 mg
Potassium	105 mg
Iron	1 mg
Calcium	116 mg

Turkey Pizza

Calories	84
Protein	7.5 g
Carbohydrate	9.5 g
Fiber	.5 g
Sugar	1.2 g
Fat	1.9 g
Cholesterol	15.5 mg
Saturated Fat	.9 g
Mono Fat	.5 g
Poly Fat	.2 g
Folate	6 Ug
Vitamin C	1 mg
Sodium	172 mg
Potassium	88 mg
Iron	1 mg
Calcium	67 mg

Hawaiian Pizza Muffins

1 cup	chopped lean ham	250 mL
1 cup	chopped mushrooms	250 mL
8 oz.	can pineapple tidbits, drained	227 mL
½ cup	diced, partly skimmed mozzarella cheese	125 mL
¼ cup	light Parmesan cheese	50 mL
¾ cup	Tomato Sauce, divided, page 128	175 mL
2	garlic cloves, minced	2
2 tsp.	crushed oregano	10 mL
½ tsp.	red chili flakes	2 mL
2	eggs	2
½ cup	skim milk	125 mL
¼ cup	olive oil	50 mL
2 cups	all-purpose flour	500 mL
1 tbsp.	baking powder	15 mL

- Preheat oven to 350°F (180°C).
- In a large bowl, combine ham, mushrooms, pineapple, mozzarella, Parmesan, ½ cup (125 mL) tomato sauce, garlic, oregano and chili flakes.
- In a small bowl, beat eggs with a fork, blend in milk and oil. Mix into ham mixture.
- Combine flour and baking powder with ham mixture until well blended. Divide mixture among 12 muffin tins lightly sprayed with non-stick cooking spray.
- Spoon 1 tsp. (5 mL) tomato sauce over each muffin.
- Bake 25 minutes, or until lightly browned and muffins spring back when lightly touched on top.
- Remove from tins; cool on rack.
- Serve warm or muffins can be packed for a lunch or snack. Store in refrigerator or freeze.

Yield: 12 servings
Serving Size: 1 muffin
Preparation Time:
 25 minutes

Nutritional Analysis
per serving

Calories	233
Protein	14.3 g
Carbohydrate	21.3 g
Fiber	1.2 g
Sugar	3.2 g
Fat	10.1 g
Cholesterol	58.4 mg
Saturated Fat	3.4 g
Mono Fat	5.2 g
Poly Fat	.9 g
Folate	17 Ug
Vitamin C	5 mg
Sodium	600 mg
Potassium	227 mg
Iron	2 mg
Calcium	250 mg

Shrimp Foo Yung

2 cups	fresh bean sprouts	
½ cup	frozen green peas, run under cold water to thaw	
1	celery stalk, thinly sliced	
1	carrot, shredded	
2	green onions, thinly sliced	
4 oz.	can small shrimp, rinsed and drained	113 g
8	eggs	8
2 tbsp.	all-purpose flour	25 mL
2 tbsp.	oyster sauce	25 mL
½ tsp.	sesame oil	2 mL
¼ tsp.	ground ginger	1 mL
⅛ tsp.	black pepper	0.5 mL
	canola oil	

- In a large bowl, combine sprouts, peas, celery, carrot, green onions and shrimp.
- In another bowl, beat eggs, flour, oyster sauce, sesame oil, ginger and pepper for 1 minute.
- Pour egg mixture into sprouts mixture. Stir well.
- Heat a large heavy nonstick frying pan over medium to medium-low heat. Add 2 tsp. (10 mL) canola oil to coat the bottom of the frying pan.
- Using a ⅓ cup (75 mL) measure, scoop egg and vegetable mixture and pour into the pan. Fry 3 or 4 pancakes at a time.
- Using an egg turner, push any runny egg mixture back toward each pancake while cooking, to keep a pancake shape. Fry 3 minutes per side, or until browned and set.
- Keep pancakes warm in oven while cooking remaining foo yung, adding oil 1 tsp. (5 mL) at a time as needed to keep pancakes from sticking to the pan.

Yield: 4 servings (8 pancakes)

Serving Size: 2
Preparation Time: 15 minutes

Nutritional Analysis

per serving

Calories	263
Protein	20.9 g
Carbohydrate	13.6 g
Fiber	2.4 g
Sugar	3 g
Fat	13.7 g
Cholesterol	460.7 mg
Saturated Fat	3.5 g
Mono Fat	4.1 g
Poly Fat	2.5 g
Folate	109 Ug
Vitamin C	21 mg
Sodium	354 mg
Potassium	384 mg
Iron	4 mg
Calcium	97 mg

...iche

...s

...iche is quick to ...kfast dish.

		250 mL
		250 mL
		250 mL
		2
	eggs	4
1½ cups	1% milk	375 mL
2 tbsp.	melted butter	25 mL
1 tsp.	Worcestershire sauce	5 mL
½ cup	all-purpose flour	125 mL
½ tsp.	salt	2 mL
¼ tsp.	black pepper	1 mL
dash	cayenne	dash

- Preheat oven to 350°F (190°C).
- Lightly spray a 9" (22 cm) quiche dish or a deep pie plate with nonstick cooking spray.
- Sprinkle the cheese, ham, mushrooms and onion in layers.
- In a deep bowl, beat together eggs, milk, butter, Worcestershire, flour, salt, pepper and cayenne. Pour over chopped ingredients.
- Bake for 40 to 50 minutes, or until a knife inserted in the center comes out clean. Cool for 5 to 10 minutes. Serve.

Yield: 6 servings
Serving Size: 1 wedge
(⅙ of pie)
Preparation Time:
18 minutes

Nutritional Analysis
per serving

Calories	292
Protein	23.9 g
Carbohydrate	12.8 g
Fiber	.5 g
Sugar	3.4 g
Fat	15.8 g
Cholesterol	196 mg
Saturated Fat	8.1 g
Mono Fat	5.1 g
Poly Fat	1.2 g
Folate	28 Ug
Vitamin C	3 mg
Sodium	943 mg
Potassium	362 mg
Iron	2 mg
Calcium	282 mg

Lunches, At Home & Portable

Broiled Tuna and Egg Bagel, page 64

Cabbage and Potato Soup, page 36

Scotch Egg Loaf

The traditional Scotch eggs are deep fried. This tasty attractive loaf version retains the flavor and reduces the fat.

1½ lbs.	bulk pork sausage meat	750 g
1 cup	oatmeal	250 mL
6	hard-boiled eggs, shelled	6
2 tbsp.	maple syrup	25 mL
2 tsp.	prepared mustard	10 mL

- Preheat oven to 350°F (180°C).
- In a bowl, mix pork sausage meat with oatmeal.
- Pack half of the meat mixture into a 2½ x 5 x 9" (6 x 12 x 22 cm) loaf pan.
- Roll eggs in flour to coat. Lay the eggs in 2 staggered rows lengthwise in pan. Press eggs down firmly in place.
- With fingers, pack remaining meat mixture around and on top of eggs to completely cover.
- Bake the loaf for 45 minutes.
- In a small bowl, stir together the maple syrup and mustard. Drizzle the sauce over the loaf; return it to the oven for 3 minutes.
- Remove the loaf from the oven and let it rest for 15 minutes.
- Remove the loaf from the loaf pan; place on a serving plate.
- Cut into 8, 1" (2.5 cm) slices.

Serve with Potato Pancakes, page 19, and applesauce.

Yield: 8 servings

Serving Size: 1"
(2.5 cm) slice
Preparation Time:
10 minutes

Nutritional Analysis

per serving

Calories	273
Protein	14.9 g
Carbohydrate	13.1 g
Fiber	1.5 g
Sugar	4.4 g
Fat	17.4 g
Cholesterol	195 mg
Saturated Fat	5.7 g
Mono Fat	7.4 g
Poly Fat	2.4 g
Folate	21 Ug
Vitamin C	1 mg
Sodium	584 mg
Potassium	250 mg
Iron	2 mg
Calcium	44 mg

Hamburger Cups

Very versatile, these can be eaten cold as a portable lunch with a cup of soup. Hamburger cups can be frozen, thawed then reheated in the oven.

12	slices whole-wheat bread, trim off ¼" (6 mm) of crust*	12
1 lb.	lean ground beef	500 g
1	egg	1
½, 1½ oz.	pkg. onion soup mix	½, 42 g
½ cup	grated Cheddar cheese	125 mL
⅓ cup	dry bread crumbs	75 mL
¼ cup	finely chopped onion	50 mL
½ tsp.	crushed oregano	2 mL

- Preheat oven to 350°F (180°C).
- Lightly spray muffin tins with nonstick cooking spray.
- Press a bread slice into each muffin cup.
- In a medium bowl, mix together ground beef, egg, onion soup mix, cheese, bread crumbs, onion and oregano.
- Divide meat mixture into 12 portions using a ¼ cup (50 mL) measure. Roll into meatballs.
- Press 1 meatball into each bread cup.
- If short on the last meatball, pinch from the others to make up.
- Bake the cups in the bottom third of the oven for 40 to 45 minutes, until hamburger feels firm when pressed on top and no pink juice appears.
- Remove hamburger cups from tins to a rack and cool for several minutes before serving.

* Save crusts for Bread Fries on page 73.

Yield: 12 servings
Serving Size: 1 cup (250 mL)
Preparation Time: 65 minutes

Nutritional Analysis
per serving

Calories	205
Protein	13.7 g
Carbohydrate	14.8 g
Fiber	2.1 g
Sugar	1.3 g
Fat	10.2 g
Cholesterol	52.2 mg
Saturated Fat	4.1 g
Mono Fat	4.2 g
Poly Fat	7 g
Folate	20 Ug
Vitamin C	0 mg
Sodium	368 mg
Potassium	181 mg
Iron	2 mg
Calcium	68 mg

Bread Fries

These "fries" are great for dipping with soups or salsa or just the way they are.

- With the crusts trimmed from the bread in the Hamburger Cups recipe, page 72, make "bread fries" for the kids.
- Bake the "fries" while you are preparing the hamburger cups.
- Lay the crusts on a baking sheet. Spray crusts lightly with nonstick cooking spray.
- Sprinkle lightly with garlic salt, taco seasoning or whatever you prefer.
- Bake at 350°F (180°C) for 12 minutes, or until crispy and browned.

Nutrition Tips:

Tips for sensible drinking:
- Drink water at frequent intervals throughout the day; before, during, and after exercise.
- Choose a drink that you enjoy, e.g., water, fruit juices, etc. Cool drinks are usually more refreshing.
- Choose a drink which meets your needs. Remember that taking extra carbohydrate drinks won't help you if your stores are at risk.
- Start drinking early. Don't wait until you feel thirsty – by this time you are already dehydrated.
- Drink to replace your fluid losses after exercise. Observe the color of your urine, it should be pale.
- If celebrating after an event, be sure to rehydrate fully before drinking alcohol.
- Alcohol, tea, coffee, and other caffeine containing beverages should not be consumed precompetition as they stimulate urine output and effectively dehydrate the body.

Yield: 12 servings (48 Bread Fries)
Serving Size:
4 Bread Fries

Nutritional Analysis
per serving

Calories	32
Protein	1.2 g
Carbohydrate	6 g
Fiber	.9 g
Sugar	.6 g
Fat	.5 g
Cholesterol	0 mg
Saturated Fat	.1 g
Mono Fat	.2 g
Poly Fat	.1 g
Folate	6 Ug
Vitamin C	0 mg
Sodium	169 mg
Potassium	32 mg
Iron	0 mg
Calcium	9 mg

Sloppy Joes

Family and crowd pleasers, Sloppy Joes combine easy preparation and on-hand ingredient convenience with great flavor.

1 lb.	lean ground beef	500 g
½	medium onion, chopped	½
2	celery stalks, sliced	2
10 oz.	can mushrooms stems and pieces, drained	284 mL
1 cup	frozen OR canned kernel corn	250 mL
14 oz.	can beans in molasses	398 mL
10 oz.	can tomato soup	284 mL
⅔ cup	water	150 mL
2 tbsp.	Worcestershire sauce	25 mL
2 tsp.	soy sauce	10 mL
1 tbsp.	brown sugar	15 mL
¼ tsp.	black pepper	1 mL

- Sauté beef over medium heat in a nonstick frying pan until all pink is gone, about 12 minutes. Blot any excess fat from the frying pan and the beef with paper towel.
- Add onion and celery. Reduce heat to medium low. Cook for 5 minutes, stirring occasionally.
- Add mushrooms, corn, beans, tomato soup, water, Worcestershire, soy sauce, brown sugar and pepper. Stir.
- Cover and simmer gently for 30 minutes.
- Serve on a thick slice of lightly toasted sourdough bread.

Yield: 6 servings
Serving Size: ¾ cup (175 mL)
Preparation Time: 25 minutes

Nutritional Analysis
per serving

Calories	396
Protein	27.2 g
Carbohydrate	32.9 g
Fiber	6.5 g
Sugar	12.9 g
Fat	18.2 g
Cholesterol	86.1 mg
Saturated Fat	7.8 g
Mono Fat	7.4 g
Poly Fat	.9 g
Folate	63 Ug
Vitamin C	26 mg
Sodium	757 mg
Potassium	808 mg
Iron	4 mg
Calcium	81 mg

Beef and Broccoli Pies

2 tbsp.	butter	25 mL
2 tbsp.	all-purpose flour	25 mL
¾ cup	1% milk	175 mL
1 cup	grated sharp Cheddar cheese	250 mL
1 tsp.	dry mustard	5 mL
1 tsp.	Worcestershire sauce	5 mL
¼ tsp.	salt	1 mL
¼ tsp.	black pepper	1 mL
2 cups	chopped broccoli, steamed tender-crisp and cooled	500 mL
1 cup	chopped roast beef	250 mL
2 cups	all-purpose flour	500 mL
2 tsp.	baking powder	10 mL
1 tsp.	salt	5 mL
¼ cup	shortening	50 mL
½ cup	1% milk	125 mL

- In a saucepan, over medium heat, melt butter. Add 2 tbsp. (30 mL) flour, stirring well. Slowly stir in milk until smooth. Cook until thickened.
- Reduce heat to medium-low. Add cheese, mustard, Worcestershire, salt and pepper. Stir well.
- Add broccoli and beef. Remove from heat and let cool.
- Preheat oven to 375°F (190°C).
- In a bowl, combine flour, baking powder and salt.
- Add shortening, blend with a pastry blender.
- Slowly add milk; mix with a fork until dough forms a ball.
- Knead dough about 20 times on a floured surface.
- Cut dough into 8 pieces. Roll each piece into a 6" (15 cm) circle.
- Place a ¼ cup (50 mL) scoop of filling on circles.
- Dampen edges with water and fold circles in half. Seal edges with a fork; prick 3 to 5 holes in tops.
- Bake 20 to 25 minutes, or until golden brown.
- To serve, reheat in a microwave or oven.

Yield: 8 servings

Serving Size: 1 pie
Preparation Time: 45 minutes

Nutritional Analysis

per serving

Calories	320
Protein	13.5 g
Carbohydrate	29.7 g
Fiber	2.1 g
Sugar	3.1 g
Fat	16.2 g
Cholesterol	33.9 mg
Saturated Fat	7.3 g
Mono Fat	5 g
Poly Fat	2 g
Folate	34 Ug
Vitamin C	31 mg
Sodium	616 mg
Potassium	278 mg
Iron	3 mg
Calcium	266 mg

Mexican Pizza

A whole-wheat, cornmeal and herb crust is enhanced with colorful peppers, tomato and chili beef toppings.

Whole-Wheat, Cornmeal Crust

¾ cup	whole-wheat flour	175 mL
½ cup	all-purpose flour	125 mL
½ cup	cornmeal	125 mL
1 tsp.	baking powder	5 mL
½ tsp.	baking soda	2 mL
½ tsp.	seasoning salt	2 mL
½ tsp.	crushed oregano	2 mL
¼ tsp.	granulated garlic	1 mL
¾ cup	plain yogurt	175 mL
2 tbsp.	olive oil	25 mL

Chili Beef Topping

1 lb.	lean ground beef	500 g
1	garlic clove, minced	1
1 tsp.	chili powder	5 mL
½ tsp.	seasoning salt	2 mL
½ tsp.	crushed oregano	2 mL
¼ tsp.	cumin	1 mL
¼ cup	diced onion	50 mL
¼ cup	taco sauce	50 mL
7	green pepper rings	7
1	large tomato, diced	1
¼ cup	sliced black olives	50 mL
1 cup	shredded Monterey Jack cheese	250 mL

- To prepare the crust, in a large bowl, stir together whole-wheat flour, all-purpose flour, cornmeal, baking powder, baking soda, seasoning salt, oregano and garlic.
- Combine yogurt with oil, pour over flour mixture. Mix well with a fork.
- Knead dough a few times on a floured surface. Cover while making the topping.

Mexican Pizza

continued

- To prepare the topping; in a medium nonstick frying pan, over medium-low heat, fry beef and garlic, breaking up well. Cook for 15 minutes, until beef starts to brown and is no longer pink.
- Sprinkle with chili powder, seasoning salt, oregano, cumin and onion. Stir and cook for 1 minute.
- Tilt pan to drain off any liquid with a spoon or paper towel. Remove from heat.
- Preheat oven to 425°F (220°C).
- On a floured surface, roll out dough to a 12" (30 cm) circle, ¼" (6 mm) thick.
- Transfer dough to a pizza pan or baking sheet lightly greased with olive oil.
- Spread taco sauce over crust.
- Sprinkle cooked ground beef and onion over. Lay pepper rings around inner edge of pizza and 1 ring in the middle.
- Sprinkle with diced tomato and black olive slices. Sprinkle cheese on top.
- Bake on bottom rack for 20 minutes, or until bottom of crust is beginning to brown and cheese is melted.

Variations: Serve with a dollop of sour cream if you like. For those who like it hot, sliced jalapeños or crushed hot chili flakes can be added before cooking.

Yield:

4 servings

Serving Size: 2 slices
Preparation time:
  40 minutes

Nutritional Analysis

per serving

Calories	725
Protein	42.7 g
Carbohydrate	51.6 g
Fiber	5.7 g
Sugar	4.9 g
Fat	39.2 g
Cholesterol	118.5 mg
Saturated Fat	14.3 g
Mono Fat	16.9 g
Poly Fat	2.1 g
Folate	49 Ug
Vitamin C	20 mg
Sodium	687 mg
Potassium	905 mg
Iron	5 mg
Calcium	410 mg

Curried Beef Packets

1 lb.	lean ground beef	500 g
½ cup	diced onion	125 mL
2	garlic cloves, minced	2
1	medium potato, ¼" (6 mm) cubes	1
½ tsp.	curry powder, more to taste	2 mL
½ tsp.	chili powder	2 mL
½ tsp.	ground coriander	2 mL
½ tsp.	turmeric	2 mL
½ cup	beef stock, page 44	125 mL
½ cup	frozen green peas	125 mL
2 tbsp.	tomato paste	25 mL
6, 10"	flour tortillas	6, 25 cm
4 tsp.	canola oil, divided	20 mL

- In a medium nonstick frying pan, over medium heat, brown beef, onion and garlic for 10 minutes. Drain off fat. Add potato, curry, chili powder, coriander and turmeric. Stir for 1 minute.
- Add beef stock, stir and cover. Reduce heat to medium low; cook for 10 minutes.
- Stir in peas. Cover; cook for 15 minutes; stir occasionally until potato is cooked. Stir in tomato paste.
- Remove from heat and cool for 15 minutes.
- Lay a tortilla flat; place ½ cup (125 mL) filling on top. Bring bottom of tortilla up ⅔ of the way; fold in sides, holding firm. Roll bottom up and over, forming a packet. Repeat with remaining 5.
- Heat a large, heavy nonstick pan on medium low; add 2 tsp. (10 mL) of oil. Place 3 packets in pan, seam side down. Press on tops to flatten slightly. Fry until golden, 1½ minutes. Turn; repeat on other side. Remove and keep warm in oven.
- Heat remaining 2 tsp. (10 mL) of oil in the frying pan and fry the last 3 packets. Serve immediately. To reheat, use the microwave

Serve with sweet mango chutney or plain yogurt mixed with mint sauce.

Yield: 6 servings
Serving Size: 1 packet
Preparation Time:
1 hour 15 minutes

Nutritional Analysis
per serving

Calories	357
Protein	16.9 g
Carbohydrate	38.2 g
Fiber	3.4 g
Sugar	2 g
Fat	14.9 g
Cholesterol	37.5 mg
Saturated Fat	3.9 g
Mono Fat	7 g
Poly Fat	2.7 g
Folate	23 Ug
Vitamin C	6 mg
Sodium	358 mg
Potassium	370 mg
Iron	3 mg
Calcium	81 mg

Portable Snacks

Healthy Eating for Healthy Lifestyles

Stuffed Celery Sticks

2	celery stalks, trimmed, washed, well dried	2
2 tbsp.	light cream cheese	25 mL
2 tbsp.	finely grated carrot	25 mL
2 tbsp.	chopped raisins	25 mL

- In a small bowl, mash the cream cheese and carrot with a fork. Stir in raisins.
- With a spoon, fill celery cavities, dividing filling between the 2 stalks.
- Cut stalks in half crosswise.
- Wrap in waxed paper.

Note: Celery sticks will keep up to 1 day in the refrigerator.

Yield: 2 servings
Serving Size: 2 pieces
Preparation Time: 10 minutes

Nutritional Analysis
per serving

Calories	72
Protein	2.2 g
Carbohydrate	10.4 g
Fiber	1.2 g
Sugar	7.7 g
Fat	2.6 g
Cholesterol	7.5 mg
Saturated Fat	1.8 g
Mono Fat	0 g
Poly Fat	0 g
Folate	15 Ug
Vitamin C	4 mg
Sodium	113 mg
Potassium	233 mg
Iron	0 mg
Calcium	42 mg

Cheddar-Stuffed Apple

1	apple	1
3 tbsp.	grated Cheddar cheese	45 mL
1 tbsp.	light cream cheese	15 mL
1 tbsp.	chopped walnuts	15 mL
1	walnut half	1

- Wash and core apple.
- In a small bowl, cream Cheddar and cream cheese together.
- Stir in walnuts.
- Pack cheese mixture into cored apple top. Top with walnut half.
- Wrap in plastic wrap to transport.

Yield: 1 serving
Serving Size: 1 apple
Preparation Time: 4 minutes

Nutritional Analysis
per serving

Calories	265
Protein	9.6 g
Carbohydrate	23.5 g
Fibre	4.3 g
Sugar	20 g
Fat	16 g
Cholesterol	29.8 mg
Saturated Fat	6.7 g
Mono Fat	3.3 g
Poly Fat	4.3 g
Folate	17 Ug
Vitamin C	8 mg
Sodium	207 mg
Potassium	262 mg
Iron	1 mg
Calcium	189 mg

Fruit Kebobs

6 cups	assorted fruit* in cubes or balls (choose 4 to 6 fruits such as watermelon, honeydew, cantaloupe, strawberries, kiwi, oranges, grapefruit, pineapple, red OR green grapes – 48 pieces in total)	1.5 L
6, 8"	wooden skewers	6, 20 cm
2 tbsp.	fresh lime juice	25 mL
2 tbsp.	liquid honey	25 mL
1 tbsp.	chopped fresh mint OR 1 tsp. (15 mL) dried	15 mL
¼ tsp.	ground ginger	1 mL

- Prepare fruit in balls or chunks.
- Alternately thread 8 pieces of fruit on each skewer.
- Lay skewers in a 9 x 13" (22 x 34 cm) baking dish.
- In a small bowl, combine lime juice, honey, mint and ginger. Stir well.
- Drizzle marinade over kebabs. Marinate, refrigerated, for up to 4 hours before serving.

Note: If packing for a portable snack, cut sharp tips off skewers. Wrap kebabs in heavy foil wrap or place in a heavy sealable storage bag.

* The fruits used in the nutritional analysis were, 1 banana, 1 orange, 5 sliced strawberries, 1 kiwi.

Yield: 6 servings
Serving Size: 1 kebab
Preparation Time:
  22 minutes

Nutritional Analysis
per serving

Calories	123
Protein	1.6 g
Carbohydrate	30.7 g
Fiber	4.2 g
Sugar	25.6 g
Fat	.7 g
Cholesterol	0 mg
Saturated Fat	.1 g
Mono Fat	.1 g
Poly Fat	.3 g
Folate	43 Ug
Vitamin C	121 mg
Sodium	8 mg
Potassium	499 mg
Iron	1 mg
Calcium	39 mg

Candied Orange Peel

Candied peel is delicious and decorative. Eat as is or chop to add to baking or sprinkle on cakes, etc.

2	oranges, rind of	2
1 cup	granulated sugar	250 mL
4	whole allspice OR cloves	4
4 slices	fresh ginger (optional)	4 slices
¼ cup	granulated sugar	50 mL

- Score the peel of the oranges into quarters, remove carefully with fingers.
- Bring the orange peel and 4 cups (1 L) of water to a boil.
- Reduce heat and simmer for 30 minutes.
- Drain and repeat the process. Drain. Reserve ½ cup (125 mL) of orange water.
- With a spoon, gently scrape the white part off the peel. Cut the peel lengthwise into ¼" (6 mm) strips.
- In a small saucepan, over medium-high heat, combine the orange water, 1 cup (250 mL) sugar, allspice and ginger.
- Bring to a boil, stirring until sugar is dissolved.
- Add peel; reduce heat and simmer for 45 minutes, stirring frequently.
- Turn peel mixture into a strainer and drain well.
- Put sugar on a sheet of waxed paper. Turn peel onto sugar.
- Toss peel quickly to coat. Remove peel to the side of the waxed paper to dry.

Yield: 6 servings (24 strips – 1 cup [250 mL])
Serving Size: 4 strips (¼ cup [50 mL])
Preparation Time: 10 minutes

Nutritional Analysis
per serving

Calories	163
Protein	0 g
Carbohydrate	42 g
Fiber	.1 g
Sugar	40.4 g
Fat	0 g
Cholesterol	0 mg
Saturated Fat	0 g
Mono Fat	0 g
Poly Fat	0 g
Folate	0 Ug
Vitamin C	0 mg
Sodium	1 mg
Potassium	7 mg
Iron	0 mg
Calcium	2 mg

Apple Roll Up Sandwich

2, 8"	whole-wheat tortillas	2, 20 cm
¼ cup	cottage cheese	50 mL
1 tbsp.	peanut butter	15 mL
1 tsp.	honey	5 mL
dash	cinnamon	dash
1	small apple	1

- Lay 2 tortillas on a flat surface.
- In a small bowl, combine cottage cheese, peanut butter, honey and cinnamon. Stir well.
- Divide the cottage cheese mixture and spread half on each tortilla.
- Core and quarter the apple. Thinly slice the apple and arrange half of the slices on each tortilla.
- Roll up tortillas tightly, tucking in apple as you roll.
- Wrap each roll separately in waxed paper and refrigerate.

Variations: Use raisins and bananas. Eat tortillas whole as a sandwich or cut into 1" (2.5 cm) rounds.

Yield: 2 servings
Serving Size:
  1 sandwich
Preparation Time:
  10 minutes

Nutritional Analysis
per serving

Calories	232
Protein	9 g
Carbohydrate	34.2 g
Fiber	3.3 g
Sugar	12.4 g
Fat	7.2 g
Cholesterol	2.4 mg
Saturated Fat	1.5 g
Mono Fat	3.1 g
Poly Fat	2.2 g
Folate	16 Ug
Vitamin C	3 mg
Sodium	320 mg
Potassium	202 mg
Iron	1 mg
Calcium	70 mg

Nutrition Tips:

Each time you exercise muscle, glycogen becomes somewhat depleted. By eating a high carbohydrate diet, it is likely that you will replenish glycogen stores, thereby allowing for another hard bout of training the following day.

Fruit and Nut Bagel

1	large cinnamon raisin bagel	1
¼ cup	light cream cheese	50 mL
¼ cup	chopped dried fruit (apple, peach, prunes, etc.)	50 mL
1 tsp.	honey	5 mL
2 tbsp.	chopped walnuts	25 mL

- Cut bagel in half horizontally.
- In a small bowl, combine cream cheese, dried fruit and honey. Mix well.
- Divide mixture between bagel halves: smooth out. Sprinkle 1 tbsp. (15 mL) of walnuts on each.
- Wrap each half in waxed paper.

Yield: 2 servings
Serving Size: ½ bagel
Preparation time:
   8 minutes

Nutritional Analysis
per serving

Calories	275
Protein	8.9 g
Carbohydrate	38.6 g
Fiber	2.5 g
Sugar	19.5 g
Fat	10.1 g
Cholesterol	15 mg
Saturated Fat	3.9 g
Mono Fat	1.1 g
Poly Fat	3.2 g
Folate	18 Ug
Vitamin C	1 mg
Sodium	266 mg
Potassium	313 mg
Iron	2 mg
Calcium	60 mg

Crunchy Peanut Butter Fingers

½ cup	honey	125 mL
⅓ cup	lightly packed brown sugar	75 mL
1 tbsp.	molasses	15 mL
1 cup	peanut butter	250 mL
2 cups	corn flakes	500 mL
1 cup	grape nuts cereal	250 mL
1 cup	crispy rice cereal	250 mL

- In a large microwave-safe bowl, heat honey, sugar and molasses on Low 2 minutes, 30 seconds, stirring once halfway through.
- Add peanut butter, blend well.
- Add corn flakes, grape nuts and rice cereal. Mix well to coat.
- Pat into a 7 x 11" (17 x 28 cm) rectangular pan sprayed with nonstick cooking spray. Let cool ½ hour before slicing into 22, 1 x 3½" (2.5 x 8.5 cm) fingers. Store in the refrigerator.

Yield: 22 servings
Serving Size: 1 bar, 1 x
   3½" (2.5 x 8.5 cm)
Preparation Time:
   11 minutes

Nutritional Analysis
per serving

Calories	140
Protein	3.8 g
Carbohydrate	20.1 g
Fiber	1.4 g
Sugar	11.3 g
Fat	5.9 g
Cholesterol	0 mg
Saturated Fat	1.1 g
Mono Fat	2.7 g
Poly Fat	1.7 g
Folate	22 Ug
Vitamin C	1 mg
Sodium	130 mg
Potassium	153 mg
Iron	2 mg
Calcium	16 mg

Granola

Versatile and flavorful, use this granola as a dry cereal with milk; sprinkle on yogurt or fruit salad and use in baking.

4 cups	oatmeal	1 L
2 cups	raw wheat germ	500 mL
½ cup	raw, shelled sunflower seeds	125 mL
½ cup	unsweetened, shredded coconut	125 mL
½ cup	flaked, natural almonds	125 mL
¼ cup	raw sesame seeds	50 mL
½ cup	honey	125 mL
⅓ cup	canola oil	75 mL
1 cup	raisins OR mixed dried berries	250 mL

- Preheat oven to 300°F (150°C).
- In a 9 x 13" (22 x 34 cm) baking pan, mix together oatmeal, wheat germ, sunflower seeds, coconut, almonds and sesame seeds.
- In a small saucepan, melt honey and oil. Stir. Pour over oatmeal mixture and mix until well coated.
- Bake for 45 minutes, or until golden, stirring every 15 minutes.
- Remove from oven; stir in raisins or dried berries.

Yield: 27 servings
Serving Size: ⅓ cup (75 mL)
Preparation Time: 10 minutes

Nutritional Analysis

per serving

Calories	182
Protein	5.6 g
Carbohydrate	23.9 g
Fiber	2.7 g
Sugar	10.7 g
Fat	8.1 g
Cholesterol	0 mg
Saturated Fat	1.2 g
Mono Fat	1.4 g
Poly Fat	2.8 g
Folate	34 Ug
Vitamin C	0 mg
Sodium	28 mg
Potassium	212 mg
Iron	1 mg
Calcium	30 mg

Nutrition Tips:

Carbonated beverages are not a good choice the day of an event because the fizz inhibits the amount one would drink to restore fluids, in addition to causing stomach bloating during exercise.

Chinese Snack Mix

½ lb.	whole blanched almonds	250 g
1 tbsp.	margarine, melted	15 mL
2 tbsp.	teriyaki sauce	25 mL
2 cups	rice crackers*	500 mL
1½ cups	dry chow mein noodles	375 mL
2, 1¼ oz.	sesame bars, cut OR chopped into ¼" (6 mm) squares	2, 35 g
4 oz.	candied pineapple, chopped (about ½ cup [125 mL])	113 g
2 tbsp.	finely chopped crystallized ginger	25 mL

- Preheat oven to 300°F (150°C).
- In a medium bowl, toss almonds with margarine and teriyaki sauce.
- Pour almonds onto a baking sheet.
- Bake for 25 minutes, stirring occasionally, until almonds are browned.
- Remove the almond mixture from the oven and spoon onto paper towels to cool.
- In a large heavy storage bag, toss together cooled almonds, rice crackers, chow mein noodles, sesame bars, pineapple and ginger.

* Rice crackers are small puffed rice shapes usually found in the bulk section or cracker and cookie sections of grocery stores.

Yield: 11 servings
Serving Size: ½ cup (125 mL)
Preparation Time: 20 minutes

Portable Snacks

Berry Nutrition Bars, page 92

"Whatever" Cookies, page 94

Apple Pie Muffins, page 98

Nutritional Analysis
per serving

Calories	259
Protein	7.8 g
Carbohydrate	31.6 g
Fiber	2.6 g
Sugar	1.9 g
Fat	13.5 g
Cholesterol	0 mg
Saturated Fat	1.2 g
Mono Fat	7.6 g
Poly Fat	3.9 g
Folate	2 Ug
Vitamin C	11 mg
Sodium	322 mg
Potassium	387 mg
Iron	3 mg
Calcium	86 mg

Caramel Corn and Peanuts

16 cups	air-popped popcorn	4 L
½ cup	margarine OR butter	125 mL
1 cup	brown sugar	250 mL
½ cup	corn syrup	125 mL
¼ cup	molasses	50 mL
½ tsp.	salt	2 mL
1 tsp.	caramel extract OR vanilla extract	5 mL
½ tsp.	baking soda	2 mL
2 cups	Spanish peanuts	500 mL

- Preheat oven to 250°F (120°C).
- Place popcorn in a large roaster sprayed with nonstick cooking spray.
- Melt margarine in a medium saucepan over medium heat.
- Stir in brown sugar, corn syrup, molasses and salt.
- Bring to a boil, and boil for 12 to 14 minutes, stirring occasionally.
- Boil hard without stirring for 5 minutes. Remove from the heat; stir in the caramel extract and baking soda. Stir well.
- Gradually pour syrup over popcorn; sprinkle peanuts over and mix well.
- Bake for 1 hour, stirring every 15 minutes.
- Remove the popcorn from the oven and turn it immediately onto waxed paper. Cool the popcorn completely.
- Break caramel corn into pieces. Store in tightly covered containers.

Variation: For those wanting a lighter flavor, increase corn syrup to ¾ cup (175 mL) and delete the molasses.

Yield: 18 servings
Serving Size: 1 cup
(250 mL)
Preparation Time:
15 minutes

Nutritional Analysis
per serving

Calories	252
Protein	4.7 g
Carbohydrate	30.9 g
Fiber	2.4 g
Sugar	18.1 g
Fat	13.4 g
Cholesterol	0 mg
Saturated Fat	2 g
Mono Fat	6.1 g
Poly Fat	4.6 g
Folate	26 Ug
Vitamin C	0 mg
Sodium	315 mg
Potassium	312 mg
Iron	1 mg
Calcium	55 mg

Sweet Cinnamon Nuts

1	egg white	1
1 cup	unsalted pretzels	250 mL
½ cup	shelled walnuts	125 mL
½ cup	pecan halves	125 mL
½ cup	whole blanched almonds	125 mL
½ cup	unsalted shelled peanuts	125 mL
¼ cup	granulated sugar	50 mL
1 tsp.	cinnamon	5 mL
½ tsp.	ground ginger	2 mL
⅛ tsp.	ground nutmeg	0.5 mL
⅛ tsp.	ground cloves	0.5 mL

- Preheat oven to 300°F (150°C).
- In a bowl, beat egg white until white and foamy.
- Add pretzels, walnuts, pecans, almonds and peanuts. Toss to coat.
- In a small bowl, combine sugar, cinnamon, ginger, nutmeg and cloves. Sprinkle over nuts. Toss to coat.
- Spread nut mixture in a single layer on an ungreased baking sheet.
- Bake for 30 minutes, or until browned.
- Remove nuts from the oven, loosen with a spatula. Cool on waxed paper.

Nutrition Tips:

Sports drinks are not required for any activity under 60 minutes. They do not provide a balance of nutrients and should not normally replace food. However, in situations where athletes are unable to eat, they can provide a useful source of energy (e.g., When exercising before breakfast; between events of a tournament; immediately after exercise.)

Yield: 10 servings
Serving Size: ⅓ cup (75 mL)
Preparation Time: 10 minutes

Nutritional Analysis
per serving

Calories	193
Protein	6.4 g
Carbohydrate	13.3 g
Fiber	2.1 g
Sugar	5.9 g
Fat	14.2 g
Cholesterol	0 mg
Saturated Fat	1.3 g
Mono Fat	7.2 g
Poly Fat	5.2 g
Folate	16 Ug
Vitamin C	0 mg
Sodium	82 mg
Potassium	154 mg
Iron	1 mg
Calcium	36 mg

Energy Nuggets

¾ cup	liquid honey	175 mL
¼ cup	cooking molasses	50 mL
½ cup	peanut butter	125 mL
1 cup	oatmeal	250 mL
¾ cup	skim milk powder	175 mL
½ cup	chocolate chips, chopped	125 mL
½ cup	wheat germ	125 mL
½ cup	crushed peanuts	125 mL
½ cup	raisins, chopped	125 mL
2 tbsp.	flax seed	25 mL
60	4 x 4" (10 x 10 cm) squares of waxed paper	60

- In a large bowl, combine honey, molasses and peanut butter. Stir well.
- Add oatmeal, milk powder, chocolate chips, wheat germ, peanuts, raisins and flax seed. Mix well.
- Chill for 15 minutes.
- Lay out 12 squares of waxed paper at a time on a counter.
- Using a sturdy dessert spoon, scoop out a 2 tsp.- (10 mL) sized portion of the oatmeal mixture. Place on waxed paper.
- Continue with the rest.
- Rinse hands, roll up waxed paper around each nugget. Twist ends to close.
- Repeat process until done. Store in the refrigerator.

Yield: 30 servings (60 nuggets)
Serving Size: 2 nuggets
Preparation Time: 1 hour

Nutritional Analysis
per serving

Calories	147
Protein	4 g
Carbohydrate	20.7 g
Fiber	1.4 g
Sugar	15.4 g
Fat	6.2 g
Cholesterol	1.2 mg
Saturated Fat	1.8 g
Mono Fat	2.6 g
Poly Fat	1.6 g
Folate	18 Ug
Vitamin C	0 mg
Sodium	70 mg
Potassium	250 mg
Iron	1 mg
Calcium	61 mg

Berry Nutrition Bars

¾ cup	buttermilk*	175 mL
1	egg	1
⅓ cup	canola oil	75 mL
1½ cups	all-purpose flour	375 mL
1¼ cups	finely chopped strawberries	300 mL
1 cup	chopped raisins	250 mL
½ cup	toasted slivered almonds	125 mL
½ cup	dried blueberries	125 mL
1¼ cups	fruit and nut granola	300 mL
½ cup	brown sugar	125 mL
2 tsp.	grated lemon rind	10 mL
1 tsp.	baking powder	5 mL
1 tsp.	baking soda	5 mL
½ tsp.	cinnamon	2 mL
½ tsp.	salt	2 mL

- Preheat oven to 350°F (180°C).
- In a medium bowl, whisk together buttermilk, egg and canola oil until blended.
- In a large bowl, combine flour, strawberries, raisins, almonds, blueberries, granola, sugar, lemon rind, baking powder, baking soda, cinnamon and salt.
- Stir buttermilk mixture into flour mixture until well combined.
- Lightly spray a 9 x 13" (22 x 34 cm) baking pan with nonstick cooking spray. Pour in batter.
- Bake for 18 to 22 minutes, or until a toothpick inserted in the center comes out clean.
- Cool completely. Cut into 24, 2 x 2" (5 x 5 cm) squares. Store in the refrigerator in an airtight container.

* For buttermilk you may substitute: ¾ cup (175 mL) 1% milk plus 1 tbsp. (15 mL) lemon juice. Stir together and let sit for 5 minutes.

Pictured on page 87.

Yield: 24 servings
Serving Size: 1 square,
 2 x 2" (5 x 5 cm)
Preparation Time:
 25 minutes

Nutritional Analysis
per serving

Calories	132
Protein	2.7 g
Carbohydrate	21.3 g
Fiber	1.8 g
Sugar	10.3 g
Fat	4.9 g
Cholesterol	8.8 mg
Saturated Fat	.4 g
Mono Fat	1 g
Poly Fat	1.4 g
Folate	9 Ug
Vitamin C	8 mg
Sodium	126 mg
Potassium	140 mg
Iron	1 mg
Calcium	40 mg

Dried Fruit and Oat Squares

1 cup	chopped, pitted dates	250 mL
½ cup	chopped, pitted prunes	125 mL
½ cup	raisins	125 mL
1 cup	water	250 mL
2 tbsp.	lemon juice	25 mL
1 cup	rolled oats	250 mL
1 cup	whole-wheat flour	250 mL
1 cup	brown sugar, lightly packed	250 mL
½ tsp.	baking powder	2 mL
½ tsp.	salt	2 mL
½ cup	butter, softened	125 mL

- To prepare filling, combine dates, prunes, raisins, water and lemon juice in a 6-cup (1.5 L) microwave-safe bowl. Cover with plastic wrap, poke holes in the wrap to vent. Microwave at High for 5 minutes, or until boiling, stirring halfway through cooking time. Dates should be soft. Let stand, covered, for 5 minutes. Uncover; cool to lukewarm, stirring occasionally.
- To prepare crumble, combine oats, flour, brown sugar, baking powder and salt in a mixing bowl. Cut in butter until mixture is crumbly.
- Press half the crumb mixture into an 8" (20 cm) square microwave baking dish.
- Spread filling on top. Sprinkle with remaining crumbs, patting down lightly.
- Microwave at Medium-High for 9 minutes, rotating a turn every 3 minutes.
- Cover with aluminum foil. Let stand 10 minutes. Uncover; cool completely on a wire rack before cutting into squares.

Yield: 16
Serving Size: 1 square,
2 x 2" (5 x 5 cm)
Preparation Time:
55 minutes

Nutritional Analysis
per serving

Calories	206
Protein	2.4 g
Carbohydrate	37 g
Fiber	2.7 g
Sugar	24.7 g
Fat	6.6 g
Cholesterol	16.4 mg
Saturated Fat	3.9 g
Mono Fat	1.9 g
Poly Fat	.4 g
Folate	7 Ug
Vitamin C	1 mg
Sodium	153 mg
Potassium	240 mg
Iron	1 mg
Calcium	38 mg

"Whatever" Cookies

You add your favorite flavors to these versatile cookies.

1 cup	margarine	250 mL
¾ cup	brown sugar	175 mL
¾ cup	granulated sugar	175 mL
2	eggs	2
1 tsp.	vanilla	5 mL
2 cups	all-purpose flour	500 mL
½ tsp.	baking powder	2 mL
5 cups	of 5 cereals/grains/nuts	1.25 L
	"whatever"*, 1 cup (250 mL)	
	of EACH	

- Preheat oven to 350°F (180°C).
- In a large bowl, mix together margarine, brown sugar, sugar, eggs and vanilla.
- Add flour, baking powder and "whatever". Mix well.
- Drop dough by rounded teaspoonfuls (7 mL) on ungreased cookie sheets.
- Bake for 10 to 14 minutes.

* To make "whatever", combine 1 cup (250 mL) EACH of 5 assorted foodstuffs: oatmeal, granola, dried cranberries, sunflower seeds, sesame seeds, flax, bran, chopped raisins, currants, nuts, puffed rice cereal, M&Ms, coconut, chopped dates, OR whatever else you would like to add.

* Nutritional analysis of this recipe was done using, 1 cup (250 mL) EACH of oatmeal, natural bran, flax seeds, raisins, chopped dates.

Pictured on page 87.

Yield: 36 servings (72 cookies)
Serving Size: 2 cookies
Preparation Time: 18 minutes

Nutritional Analysis
per serving

Calories	169
Protein	2.7 g
Carbohydrate	25.1 g
Fiber	1.9 g
Sugar	14.1 g
Fat	7 g
Cholesterol	11.8 mg
Saturated Fat	1.2 g
Mono Fat	2.4 g
Poly Fat	3 g
Folate	18 Ug
Vitamin C	0 mg
Sodium	82 mg
Potassium	159 mg
Iron	1 mg
Calcium	29 mg

Peanut Butter and Jam Cookies

1½ cups	all-purpose flour	375 mL
½ cup	granulated sugar	125 mL
½ tsp.	baking soda	2 mL
¼ tsp.	salt	1 mL
½ cup	shortening	125 mL
½ cup	smooth peanut butter	125 mL
¼ cup	corn syrup	50 mL
1 tbsp.	milk	15 mL
½ cup	jam (strawberry, raspberry, etc.)	125 mL

- In a bowl mix flour, sugar, baking soda and salt.
- Cut in shortening and peanut butter until mixture resembles coarse meal.
- Blend in corn syrup and milk.
- Shape into a 2 x 10" (5 x 25 cm) roll; refrigerate for 30 minutes.
- Preheat oven to 350°F (180°C).
- Slice roll between ¼ to ⅛" (3 to 6 mm) thick to get 48 cookies.
- Place half the slices on an ungreased cookie sheet, put 1 tsp. (5 mL) of jam on each.
- Cover with remaining slices, seal edges with a fork.
- Bake for 12 minutes, or until golden brown.
- Cool slightly; remove to cooling rack.

Nutrition Tips:

Nutrient dense snacks are important for active people, especially children. Suggestions include: an oatmeal or fruit and fiber cookie with milk and fruit; dry cereal, nut and fruit combinations with yogurt; a bagel with cheese or peanut butter and fruit.

Yield: 12 servings (24 cookies)
Serving Size: 2 cookies
Preparation Time:
35 minutes (Chilling time 30 minutes)

Nutritional Analysis
per serving

Calories	279
Protein	4.4 g
Carbohydrate	36.6 g
Fiber	1.2 g
Sugar	20.6 g
Fat	13.6 g
Cholesterol	.1 mg
Saturated Fat	3.1 g
Mono Fat	5.2 g
Poly Fat	3.6 g
Folate	17 Ug
Vitamin C	2 mg
Sodium	163 mg
Potassium	108 mg
Iron	1 mg
Calcium	19 mg

Fig and Banana Pinwheels

Fig and Banana Filling

½ lb.	figs, chopped (about 10 whole)	250 g
1	ripe banana, mashed	1
¼ cup	water	50 mL
2 tsp.	lemon juice	10 mL
1 tsp.	grated lemon peel	5 mL
¼ cup	finely chopped walnuts	50 mL

Cookie

½ cup	butter OR margarine	125 mL
½ cup	brown sugar	125 mL
½ cup	granulated sugar	125 mL
1	egg	1
1 tsp.	vanilla extract	5 mL
1¾ cups	all-purpose flour	425 mL
½ tsp.	baking soda	2 mL

- To make the filling, in a saucepan, combine figs, banana, water, lemon juice and peel.
- Cook until fruit mixture is tender and thickened.
- Add walnuts; stir well; set aside to cool.
- To make the cookie dough, in a large bowl, beat together butter, brown sugar, sugar, egg and vanilla, until light and fluffy.
- Add flour and baking soda; mix well.
- Divide dough into 2 equal portions. On floured waxed paper, roll each portion into a 7 x 11" (17 x 28 cm) rectangle.
- Spread each rectangle with filling to ½" (1 cm) of edges. Roll up jelly roll style from long side.
- Wrap in waxed paper; refrigerate 30 minutes.
- Preheat oven to 350°F (180°C).
- Cut each roll into 30 slices, about 3 slices per 1" (2.5 cm). Place 1" (2.5 cm) apart on a baking sheet sprayed with nonstick cooking spray.
- Bake 10 to 12 minutes.

Yield: 30 servings (60 cookies)
Store in a non-airtight container.
Serving Size: 2 cookies
Preparation Time:
1 Hour 10 minutes
(40 minutes prep. time,
30 minutes stand time)

Nutritional Analysis
per serving

Calories	99
Protein	1.3 g
Carbohydrate	15 g
Fiber	.6 g
Sugar	7.8 g
Fat	3.9 g
Cholesterol	7.1 mg
Saturated Fat	.6 g
Mono Fat	1.4 g
Poly Fat	1.6 g
Folate	4 Ug
Vitamin C	1 mg
Sodium	65 mg
Potassium	62 mg
Iron	0 mg
Calcium	10 mg

Cherry and Raisin Cookies

1 cup	whole-wheat flour	250 mL
1 tsp.	baking soda	5 mL
½ tsp.	salt	2 mL
2 cups	large flake oats	500 mL
¼ cup	wheat germ	50 mL
¾ cup	margarine	175 mL
1½ cups	lightly packed brown sugar	375 mL
2	eggs	2
1 tsp.	vanilla	5 mL
½ cup	medium unsweetened coconut	125 mL
½ cup	raisins	125 mL
½ cup	chopped dried cherries	125 mL
½ cup	slivered almonds	125 mL

- Preheat oven to 350°F (180°C).
- In a medium bowl, combine flour, baking soda, salt, oats and wheat germ.
- In a large bowl, cream margarine, brown sugar, eggs and vanilla.
- Add flour mixture and mix well.
- Stir in coconut, raisins, cherries and almonds.
- Drop by teaspoonfuls (5 mL) onto a lightly greased baking sheet. Flatten slightly.
- Bake 12 minutes, or until lightly browned.

Yield: 27 servings (54 cookies)
Serving Size: 2 cookies
Preparation Time: 17 minutes

Nutritional Analysis
per serving

Calories	178
Protein	3.3 g
Carbohydrate	25.2 g
Fiber	1.9 g
Sugar	13.8 g
Fat	7.9 g
Cholesterol	15.7 mg
Saturated Fat	1.7 g
Mono Fat	3.1 g
Poly Fat	2.7 g
Folate	9 Ug
Vitamin C	0 mg
Sodium	172 mg
Potassium	166 mg
Iron	1 mg
Calcium	33 mg

Nutrition Tips:

Vitamin and mineral supplements are not necessary on a balanced diet. If you are taking supplements, note the color of your urine. If it is bright yellow, you are getting too much of a vitamin or mineral and are simply excreting it.

Apple Pie Muffins

Chunks of apple make these muffins moist and add eye appeal.

1	egg	1
½ cup	canola oil	125 mL
1½ cups	apple pie filling	375 mL
2 cups	all-purpose oat and wheat flour	500 mL
⅓ cup	packed brown sugar	75 mL
2 tsp.	baking powder	10 mL
1 tsp.	baking soda	5 mL
1 tsp.	ground cinnamon	5 mL
½ tsp.	salt	2 mL
⅛ tsp.	nutmeg	0.5 mL

- Preheat oven to 400°F (200°C).
- In a large bowl beat egg.
- Stir in oil and apple pie filling.
- In a medium bowl, combine flour, sugar, baking powder, baking soda, cinnamon, salt and nutmeg.
- Stir dry mixture into wet mixture until flour is moistened.
- Spray muffin tins with nonstick cooking spray. Fill muffin tins ¾ full.
- Bake 15 minutes, or until top of muffin bounces back to the touch.

Variation: Homemade, canned or bulk apple pie filling may be used.

Pictured on page 87.

Yield: 12 servings (12 muffins)
Serving Size: 1 muffin
Preparation Time: 20 minutes

Nutritional Analysis
per serving

Calories	204
Protein	3.3 g
Carbohydrate	27.5 g
Fiber	2.8 g
Sugar	5.8 g
Fat	10.2 g
Cholesterol	17.7 mg
Saturated Fat	.9 g
Mono Fat	.2 g
Poly Fat	2.9 g
Folate	11 Ug
Vitamin C	0 mg
Sodium	282 mg
Potassium	120 mg
Iron	1 mg
Calcium	74 mg

APPETIZERS

HEALTHY EATING FOR HEALTHY LIFESTYLES

Strawberry Cheese Dip

Use as a dip for fresh fruit, pound cake or as a spread for scones.

4 oz.	light cream cheese	125 g
½ cup	light sour cream	125 mL
½ cup	sliced strawberries	125 mL
2 tbsp.	liquid honey	25 mL
1 tbsp.	lemon juice	15 mL
½ tsp.	vanilla	2 mL

- In a food processor or blender, combine cream cheese, sour cream, strawberries, honey, lemon juice and vanilla. Process until smooth.

Variations: To make **Raspberry Cheese Dip**, substitute ¾ cup (175 mL) of fresh or frozen raspberries for the strawberries. For **Mango Cheese Dip**, use chopped ripe mango and orange juice instead of the strawberries and lemon juice. For **Tangy Lemon Cheese Dip**, use 3 tbsp. (45 mL) of frozen lemon juice concentrate, 1 tsp. (5 mL) grated lemon rind and 1 tbsp. (15 mL) finely chopped fresh mint. Omit the strawberries, lemon juice and vanilla. For **Ginger Cheese Dip**, use 2 tbsp. (30 mL) minced crystallized ginger. Omit the strawberries, lemon juice and vanilla.

Yield: 12 servings
Serving Size: 2 tbsp. (25 mL)
Preparation Time: 10 minutes

Nutritional Analysis
per serving

Calories	49
Protein	1.6 g
Carbohydrate	5.2 g
Fiber	.2 g
Sugar	4.9 g
Fat	2.4 g
Cholesterol	7.8 mg
Saturated Fat	1.7 g
Mono Fat	0 g
Poly Fat	0 g
Folate	4 Ug
Vitamin C	8 mg
Sodium	51 mg
Potassium	64 mg
Iron	0 mg
Calcium	27 mg

Zesty Tortilla Chips

4, 8"	flour tortillas	4, 20 cm
	nonstick cooking spray	
	taco seasoning	

- Preheat oven to 350°F (180°C).
- Stack tortillas, cut into 8 triangles.
- Lightly spray baking pan with nonstick cooking spray.
- Arrange tortilla triangles on pan, lightly spray triangles with nonstick cooking spray.
- Sprinkle triangles lightly with taco seasoning.
- Bake chips on the middle rack of the oven for 20 minutes, turning chips over after 10 minutes.

Variations: Different colors and flavors of tortillas, e.g., herb, sun-dried tomato, whole-wheat or plain, make interesting chips. Sprinkle chips with mixed Italian herbs, crumbled oregano, or basil to vary flavors. Sprinkle with a spice mixture like Mrs. Dash if you want a salt-free topping.

Pictured on page 105.

Yield: 4 servings
Serving Size: 8 chips
Preparation Time:
 5 minutes

Nutritional Analysis
per serving

Calories	114
Protein	3 g
Carbohydrate	19.5 g
Fiber	1.2 g
Sugar	0 g
Fat	2.5 g
Cholesterol	0 mg
Saturated Fat	.4 g
Mono Fat	1 g
Poly Fat	1 g
Folate	4 Ug
Vitamin C	0 mg
Sodium	167 mg
Potassium	46 mg
Iron	1 mg
Calcium	44 mg

Nutrition Tips:

For every pound of weight loss while exercising, drink two cups (500 mL) of water to restore hydration.

To prevent dehydration, drink at least 8 cups (2 L) of fluids each day, drink 2 cups (500 mL) 2 hours before an event, 1 cup (250 mL) a half hour before competition, and 1 to 2 mouthfuls every 15 minutes while performing.

Hummus

*This Middle-Eastern spread is very easy,
very nutritious and very tasty.*

19 oz.	can chickpeas, drained, reserve ¼ cup (50 mL) liquid	540 mL
¼ cup	peanut butter*	50 mL
2 tbsp.	lemon juice	25 mL
2	garlic cloves	2
½ tsp.	cumin	2 mL
½ tsp.	salt	2 mL
dash	cayenne	dash
	chopped parsley to garnish	

- In a food processor combine chickpeas, peanut butter, lemon juice, garlic, cumin, salt and cayenne.
- Purée, adding up to 3 tbsp. (45 mL) of reserved liquid if needed to attain a smooth consistency.
- Spoon into a bowl. Refrigerate for 30 minutes.
- Sprinkle with parsley before serving.

Serve with pita bread and vegetables for dipping.

* Tahini (sesame paste) is traditionally used in this recipe, but peanut butter is more widely available and it is a good substitute.

Yield: 7 servings
Serving Size: ¼ cup (50 mL)
Preparation Time: 15 minutes

Nutritional Analysis
per serving

Calories	139
Protein	5.7 g
Carbohydrate	18.1 g
Fiber	3.7 g
Sugar	.8 g
Fat	5.4 g
Cholesterol	0 mg
Saturated Fat	1 g
Mono Fat	2.3 g
Poly Fat	1.7 g
Folate	53 Ug
Vitamin C	5 mg
Sodium	416 mg
Potassium	196 mg
Iron	1 mg
Calcium	28 mg

Broccoli Dip

*This can also be used as a filling for a bread or tortilla roll,
to be eaten whole as a snack or cut into spirals.*

1½ cups	chopped broccoli, heads and stems	375 mL
2	green onions, chopped	2
1	garlic clove	1
¾ cup	low-fat Ranch-style salad dressing*, page 44	175 mL

- Combine broccoli, onions, garlic and salad dressing in a blender or food processor. Process until broccoli is finely minced, about 5 seconds.
- Pour into a small serving bowl. Refrigerate dip for one half hour before serving.

Serve with carrot sticks, mushroom caps or whole-grain bread cubes.

* You may use homemade or commercial salad dressing.

Yield: 10 servings

Serving Size: 2 tbsp.
 (250 mL)
Preparation Time:
 10 minutes

Nutritional Analysis

per serving

Calories	44
Protein	1 g
Carbohydrate	3.3 g
Fiber	1.3 g
Sugar	1.7 g
Fat	3.2 g
Cholesterol	0 mg
Saturated Fat	.6 g
Mono Fat	.4 g
Poly Fat	.9 g
Folate	25 Ug
Vitamin C	18 mg
Sodium	81 mg
Potassium	115 mg
Iron	0 mg
Calcium	20 mg

Nutrition Tips:

General rules of thumb for precompetition nutrition:

- The closer to the event, the less protein and fat, and the more carbohydrate you should consume.
- Ensure adequate energy.
- Try to eat early enough so the stomach is empty and comfortable when competition begins.

Fresh Tomato Salsa

Salsa is the "hottest" food condiment in North America. The spicy fresh flavor is delicious on its own with corn or tortilla chips. It can also be served with eggs, grilled chicken, burgers, fish, etc.

2	medium tomatoes, diced	2
¼ cup	finely chopped onion	50 mL
1 tbsp.	finely chopped cilantro	15 mL
1	garlic clove, crushed	1
1 tsp.	lime juice	5 mL
½ tsp.	granulated sugar	2 mL
½ tsp.	jalapeño (hot pepper) sauce, or more to taste	2 mL
¼ tsp.	salt	1 mL

- In a serving bowl, mix together tomatoes, onion, cilantro, garlic, lime juice, sugar, jalapeño sauce and salt.
- Let stand for 15 minutes for flavors to develop.

Pictured on the opposite page.

Variations: Salsas can be mixtures of vegetables, fruits and/or herbs. For a **Fruit Salsa**, add 2 diced ripe mangoes, ½ a diced red pepper, 1 tsp. (5 mL) cumin, 1 tbsp. (15 mL) canola oil, ¼ cup (50 mL) EACH red wine vinegar and lime juice to the Fresh Tomato Salsa recipe. Chill for 1 to 2 hours to let the flavors develop.

Appetizers

Fresh Tomato Salsa, page 104

Zesty Tortilla Chips, page 101

Yield: 4 servings
Serving Size: ⅓ cup (75 mL)
Preparation Time: 12 minutes

Nutritional Analysis
per serving

Calories	23
Protein	1 g
Carbohydrate	4.9 g
Fiber	.9 g
Sugar	2.5 g
Fat	.2 g
Cholesterol	0 mg
Saturated Fat	0 g
Mono Fat	0 g
Poly Fat	.1 g
Folate	11 Ug
Vitamin C	14 mg
Sodium	160 mg
Potassium	175 mg
Iron	1 mg
Calcium	12 mg

Tortilla Spirals

½ cup	light cream cheese	125 mL
¼ cup	vegetable flakes	50 mL
2 tbsp.	finely chopped fresh parsley OR	25 mL
	2 tsp. (10 mL) dried	
½ tsp.	dried dillweed	2 mL
1	coarsely grated carrot	1
1	celery stalk, minced	1
1	green onion, minced	1
1	garlic clove, crushed	2
2 tbsp.	1% milk	25 mL
4, 8"	whole-wheat	4, 20 cm
	tortillas	

- In a bowl, soften cream cheese with a fork.
- Add vegetable flakes, parsley, dillweed, carrot, celery, green onion and garlic. Stir well.
- Add milk, 1 tbsp. (15 mL) at a time, stirring well.
- Lay tortilla on a flat surface.
- Spread ¼ cup (50 mL) of filling mixture over each tortilla.
- Roll up tortillas tightly; wrap in waxed paper and refrigerate for a minimum of 1 hour or up to a day ahead.
- When ready to serve, unwrap, slice ½" (1 cm) off each end and discard. Slice each roll into 6 and arrange on a serving plate.

Yield: 6 servings

Serving Size: 4 pieces
Preparation Time:
20 minutes

Nutritional Analysis

per serving

Calories	153
Protein	4.9 g
Carbohydrate	19.5 g
Fiber	1.4 g
Sugar	2.7 g
Fat	6 g
Cholesterol	10.2 mg
Saturated Fat	2.6 g
Mono Fat	.7 g
Poly Fat	.7 g
Folate	12 Ug
Vitamin C	3 mg
Sodium	226 mg
Potassium	147 mg
Iron	1 mg
Calcium	72 mg

Bagel Chips with Tofu and Smoked Salmon Spread

Tofu and Smoked Salmon Spread

11 oz.	medium tofu	300 g
5 oz.	smoked salmon	150 g
1	green onion, chopped	1
2 tbsp.	chopped fresh dillweed	25 mL
½ tsp.	grated lemon rind	2 mL
2 tbsp.	tomato-based seafood sauce	25 mL
1 tbsp.	lemon juice	15 mL
½ tsp.	celery salt	2 mL
6 drops	hot red pepper sauce	6 drops
3	multi-grain bagels	3

- To prepare the spread; in a blender or food processor, combine tofu, salmon, onion, dillweed, grated lemon rind, seafood sauce, lemon juice, celery, salt and red pepper sauce.
- Blend for 1 minute, or until well blended. Refrigerate until using.
- To prepare the chips; using a serrated knife, hold 1 bagel on its side, slice bagel into 7 to 8 thin slices, starting with the bottom side of the bagel. When you get down to the last slice, lay the bagel flat on cutting board; carefully slice off top.
- Lay bagel slices in a single layer on a baking sheet; broil 6" (15 cm) from the heat for 1½ minutes. Turn bagels over. Broil the second side for up to 1 minute, removing any bagel chips that are browning too quickly.
- Let cool. Store in an airtight container.

Serve the chips with the salmon spread.

Note: Bagels that are a few days old work the best for slicing. A bagel holder, designed specially for slicing bagels, will help save your fingers.

Yield: 12 servings
Serving size:
  2 bagel slices
Preparation Time:
  10 minutes

Nutritional Analysis
per serving

Calories	74
Protein	5.5 g
Carbohydrate	10.1 g
Fiber	.6 g
Sugar	1.6 g
Fat	1.6 g
Cholesterol	2.7 mg
Saturated Fat	.2 g
Mono Fat	.2 g
Poly Fat	.1 g
Folate	1 Ug
Vitamin C	1 mg
Sodium	264 mg
Potassium	81 mg
Iron	1 mg
Calcium	25 mg

Roasted Garlic and Jalapeño Bean Spread

2	garlic heads, unpeeled	2
2 tbsp.	olive oil	25 mL
1	jalapeño pepper	1
19 oz.	can white kidney beans, drained	540 mL
½ tsp.	salt	2 mL

- Preheat oven to 350°F (180°C).
- Remove loose outer skin from garlic heads.
- Cut a thin slice off the tops of the heads.
- Lay a 6 x 6" (15 x 15 cm) square of tinfoil on a counter. Place garlic heads on foil. Drizzle with 1 tsp. (5 ml) olive oil.
- Lay the jalapeño beside the garlic.
- Bring the corners of the foil up, crimping and lightly twisting the corners together, but leaving some space for steam to escape.
- Bake 1 hour and 15 minutes, or until garlic is very soft when pressed.
- Remove garlic from oven; cool 5 to 10 minutes.
- Hold root end of bulb and squeeze garlic into a blender or food processor.
- Cut jalapeño in half lengthwise, discarding seeds.
- Chop pepper, being careful not to get any juice in eyes. Wash hands in soapy water after chopping pepper.
- Add the jalapeño to the garlic with the beans, 1 tbsp. plus 2 tsp. (20 mL) olive oil and salt. Blend or process until smooth.

Serve with vegetables, baguette slices or tortilla chips.

Note: Use caution when working with hot peppers. Wear rubber gloves or wash hands immediately.

Yield: 20 servings (2 cups [500 mL])
Serving Size: 2 tbsp. (25 mL)
Preparation Time: 12 minutes

Nutritional Analysis
per serving

Calories	33
Protein	1.3 g
Carbohydrate	4 g
Fiber	1.2 g
Sugar	.5 g
Fat	1.4 g
Cholesterol	0 mg
Saturated Fat	.2 g
Mono Fat	1 g
Poly Fat	.2 g
Folate	11 Ug
Vitamin C	1 mg
Sodium	157 mg
Potassium	67 mg
Iron	0 mg
Calcium	10 mg

Bruschetta

Juicy, hot toasted baguette slices soaked with a tangy tomato mixture – these are truly delicious.

2 cups	finely chopped Roma tomatoes	500 mL
½ cup	finely chopped red onion	125 mL
1-2	garlic cloves, crushed	1-2
½ cup	chopped basil	125 mL
¼ cup	chopped parsley	50 mL
¼ cup	olive oil	50 mL
1 tbsp.	balsamic vinegar	15 mL
¼ tsp.	salt	1 mL
	freshly ground pepper to taste	
1	baguette, sliced	1
	Parmesan cheese	

- In a bowl, combine tomatoes, red onion, garlic, basil, parsley, olive oil, balsamic vinegar, salt and pepper. Stir well. Let sit for 15 to 20 minutes.
- Toast baguette slices under the broiler on 1 side; turn over; spoon 1 tbsp. (15 mL) of tomato mixture onto each slice. Sprinkle with Parmesan and broil 6" (15 cm) from heat, until cheese starts to brown.

Variation: The tomato mixture can also be served in a bowl and surrounded by toasted or plain baguette slices. Spoon 1 tbsp. (15 mL) of the tomato mixture onto each slice.

Yield: 10 servings
Serving Size: ¼ cup
  (50 mL) of sauce with
  3 baguette slices
Preparation time:
  15 minutes

Nutritional Analysis
per serving

Calories	146
Protein	4.2 g
Carbohydrate	17.6 g
Fiber	1.1 g
Sugar	2.4 g
Fat	6.5 g
Cholesterol	1.9 mg
Saturated Fat	1 g
Mono Fat	4.3 g
Poly Fat	.5 g
Folate	23 Ug
Vitamin C	12 mg
Sodium	299 mg
Potassium	154 mg
Iron	1 mg
Calcium	31 mg

Lentil Nachos

19 oz.	can lentils, well drained	540 mL
¼ cup	taco sauce	50 mL
14 oz.	pkg. round nacho chips	400 g
1½ cups	marble cheese, grated	375 mL
1	large tomato, diced	1
1	green pepper, diced	1
½ cup	diced onion	125 mL
½ cup	sliced black olives	125 mL
	sour cream	
	salsa	
	other toppings of your choice, e.g., jalapeño peppers, sliced mushrooms	

- Preheat oven to 350°F (180°C).
- In a bowl, combine lentils with taco sauce. Set aside.
- Lightly spray baking sheet with nonstick cooking spray.
- Spread half the bag of nacho chips on the baking sheet.
- Sprinkle half the cheese and half the lentils over the chips.
- Spread the other half of the nacho chips on top and layer with the remaining cheese, and the tomato, green pepper, onion and black olives.
- Bake on the middle rack for 20 minutes, until cheese is melted and nachos are heated through.

Serve with sour cream and salsa for dipping.

Yield: 8 servings
Serving Size: ⅛ of pan
Preparation time:
  15 minutes

Nutritional Analysis
per serving

Calories	412
Protein	13.4 g
Carbohydrate	43.9 g
Fiber	7.4 g
Sugar	2.1 g
Fat	21.4 g
Cholesterol	22.3 mg
Saturated Fat	7 g
Mono Fat	9.7 g
Poly Fat	2.1 g
Folate	99 Ug
Vitamin C	14 mg
Sodium	496 mg
Potassium	377 mg
Iron	3 mg
Calcium	243 mg

Salad Rolls with Peanut Dipping Sauce

Peanut Dipping Sauce

2 tbsp.	hoisin sauce	25 mL
2 tbsp.	peanut butter	25 mL
2 tbsp.	warm water	25 mL
2 oz.	rice stick noodles, cooked	60 g
8	leaf lettuce leaves, washed and dried	8
2"	piece of English cucumber, julienned	5 cm
5 oz.	cooked large, ready-to-serve shrimp	150 g
¼ cup	chopped fresh basil	50 mL

- To prepare dipping sauce: in a small bowl, combine hoisin, peanut butter and warm water. Stir well.
- Lay out the lettuce leaves on a plate.
- Place noodles into a bowl. If they are sticking together, quickly run under cold water to separate. Drain.
- Place the shrimp, cucumber and basil in separate bowls.
- Set everything in the middle of the table, including the dipping sauce.
- Let everyone roll their own. To make rolls, place a lettuce leaf on your plate. Pinch some noodle strands; place on a leaf. Top with 5 to 6 cucumber sticks, 2 to 3 shrimp and 2 tsp. (10 mL) chopped basil. Roll the leaf towards the base end, tucking in noodles at the sides as you roll. Once rolled, hold firmly. Dip rolls in sauce or spoon sauce into rolls.

Yield: 4 servings
Serving Size: 2 rolls
Preparation Time:
  15 minutes

Nutritional Analysis
per serving

Calories	98
Protein	9.6 g
Carbohydrate	6.5 g
Fiber	1.2 g
Sugar	1.5 g
Fat	4.1 g
Cholesterol	0 mg
Saturated Fat	.8 g
Mono Fat	1.9 g
Poly Fat	1.2 g
Folate	32 Ug
Vitamin C	4 mg
Sodium	452 mg
Potassium	148 mg
Iron	0 mg
Calcium	46 mg

Rice, Vegetables & Pasta

Healthy Eating for Healthy Lifestyles

Basic Pilaf

You can vary this basic pilaf to suit any taste.

2 tbsp.	butter	25 mL
1 cup	long-grain rice	250 mL
2½ cups	chicken stock, page 43*	625 mL

- Melt butter in a heavy saucepan over medium heat.
- Stir in rice; sauté, stirring constantly until butter is golden and foams.
- Add stock. Bring to a boil. Cover.
- Reduce heat; simmer 25 minutes, or until rice is tender and stock is absorbed. Let stand, covered, for 10 minutes.

Variations: ½ cup (125 mL) chopped cooked fresh or frozen mixed vegetables may be added at the same time as the stock. **Herbed Pilaf** is as easy as adding 2 tbsp. (25 mL) chopped fresh herbs or 2 tsp. (10 mL) dry herbs of your choice. Chopped cooked meats or seafood can also be added, with the stock, to the basic pilaf. To add onion, sauté 1 small finely chopped onion for 2-3 minutes in the butter, before adding the rice.

* If you don't have homemade stock, use low-salt chicken bouillon according to package directions.

Seasoning Rice:

Experiment with some of the following flavorings to add interest to rice dishes:

almonds	currants	Parmesan cheese
apricots	curry powder	parsley
basil	dillweed	raisins
beef or chicken stock	garlic	saffron
	lemon	thyme
chili flakes or powder	mint	tomato
	onion	vegetable stock
cinnamon	orange	wine

Yield: 4 servings
Serving Size: ¾ cup (175 mL)
Preparation Time: 5 minutes

Nutritional Analysis
per serving

Calories	247
Protein	6.4 g
Carbohydrate	37.6 g
Fiber	.6 g
Sugar	.3 g
Fat	7.3 g
Cholesterol	16.4 mg
Saturated Fat	4.1 g
Mono Fat	2.2 g
Poly Fat	.5 g
Folate	7 Ug
Vitamin C	0 mg
Sodium	549 mg
Potassium	187 mg
Iron	2 mg
Calcium	21 mg

Cheese and Herb Mashed Potatoes

*Chives, dill and Cheddar, these potatoes taste like
deluxe stuffed baked potatoes.*

4	medium potatoes, peeled and quartered	4
2 tbsp.	milk	25 mL
¼ tsp.	salt	1 mL
½ cup	grated Cheddar cheese	125 mL
1 tbsp.	chopped dillweed	15 mL
1 tbsp.	chopped chives OR finely chopped green onion	15 mL

- Boil potatoes in lightly salted water to cover. Bring to a boil over high heat.
- Reduce heat to a simmer; cover.
- Cook 15 minutes, or until done. Drain.
- Add milk, salt and cheese. Mash until smooth.
- Stir in dillweed and chives.

Variations: Different varieties of potatoes have different flavors. Try Yukon Gold potatoes for a real treat, they have a lovely golden color and a rich buttery flavor. Mashed with chicken broth and chopped fresh or dried herbs (try basil, chives, oregano, savory, etc.) and a generous sprinkle of salt and freshly ground pepper, they are a low-fat taste treat.

Yield: 4 servings
Serving Size:
¾ cup (175 mL)
Preparation Time:
35 minutes

Nutritional Analysis
per serving

Calories	119
Protein	4.2 g
Carbohydrate	18.7 g
Fiber	1.7 g
Sugar	2 g
Fat	3.3 g
Cholesterol	10.3 mg
Saturated Fat	2.1 g
Mono Fat	.9 g
Poly Fat	.1 g
Folate	12 Ug
Vitamin C	12 mg
Sodium	162 mg
Potassium	365 mg
Iron	0 mg
Calcium	80 mg

Crispy Potato Wedges

Golden and crunchy, you can season these baked "fries" to suit your own taste. No nutritional analysis is given because the dressing and seasoning variations are your choice.

2 tbsp.	light salad dressing, your choice, e.g., Italian, Caesar, herb and garlic, etc.	25 mL
1 tbsp.	olive oil	15 mL
½ tsp.	paprika	2 mL
	seasoning*, see suggestions below	
4	medium potatoes, cut lengthwise into 8 wedges each	4

- In a large bowl mix salad dressing, olive oil, paprika and your choice of seasonings.
- Add potato wedges, toss well to coat.
- Line a cookie sheet with foil, spray lightly with cooking spray.
- Arrange potato wedges in a single layer.
- Bake for 35 minutes, or until tender, in a 400°F (200°C) oven.
- Serve with a dollop of sour cream or cottage cheese.

* Try Cajun spice mixture, taco seasoning, mixed Italian herbs, lemon pepper, seasoning salt, OR salt-free seasonings like Mrs. Dash.

Pictured on page 141.

Yield: 4 servings
Serving Size: 8 wedges
Preparation Time:
  10 minutes

Broccoli and Cheddar Stuffed Potatoes

2	large baking potatoes	2
1½ cups	chopped broccoli heads and stems	375 mL
¼ cup	1% milk	50 mL
2 tsp.	butter	10 mL
¼ tsp.	salt	1 mL
dash	black pepper	dash
½ cup	cubed Cheddar cheese, ¼" (6 mm) cubes	125 mL

- Pierce potatoes; bake in microwave on High for 5 minutes. Turn over and bake for 5 minutes more. Potatoes should be soft when gently squeezed with fingers. Let rest for 15 minutes.
- Cook broccoli in enough boiling water to cover for 2½ minutes, or until tender-crisp. Drain, rinse well under cold running water. Drain.
- Preheat oven to 350°F (180°C).
- Cut potatoes in half lengthwise. With a spoon, scoop out flesh into a bowl.
- Place potato shells on a baking sheet.
- To the potato filling, add milk, butter, salt and pepper. Mash until smooth.
- Mix in broccoli and Cheddar cubes. Divide filling evenly among the shells.
- Bake for 30 minutes.

Yield: 4 servings
Serving Size: ½ potato
Preparation Time:
 40 minutes

Nutritional Analysis
per serving

Calories	208
Protein	8.1 g
Carbohydrate	29.4 g
Fiber	4.1 g
Sugar	3.4 g
Fat	7.2 g
Cholesterol	20.9 mg
Saturated Fat	4.4 g
Mono Fat	2 g
Poly Fat	.4 g
Folate	44 Ug
Vitamin C	57 mg
Sodium	285 mg
Potassium	631 mg
Iron	2 mg
Calcium	158 mg

Spinach Pie

Feta and spinach are a classic and delicious flavor combination.

¼ cup	canola margarine, melted	50 mL
1¼ cups	fine bread crumbs	300 mL
2 tbsp.	Parmesan cheese	25 mL
10 oz.	pkg. frozen chopped spinach, thawed, water squeezed out	284 g
2	green onions, thinly sliced	2
2 cups	2% creamed cottage cheese	500 mL
¼ cup	crumbled feta cheese	50 mL
2 tbsp.	all-purpose flour	15 mL
2	eggs, beaten	2
1 tbsp.	chopped fresh dillweed OR 1 tsp. (5 mL) dried	15 mL
¼ tsp.	salt	1 mL
¼ tsp.	black pepper	2 mL

- Preheat oven to 350°F (180°C).
- In a bowl, mix melted margarine, bread crumbs and Parmesan cheese. Pat ¾ of mixture into a 9" (22 cm) pie plate.
- In another bowl, mix spinach, onion, cottage cheese, feta, flour, eggs, dillweed, salt and pepper.
- Pour spinach mixture into pie shell. Sprinkle remaining crumbs on top.
- Bake 40 minutes, or until the center looks and feels set.
- Serve warm or cold.

Yield: 6 lunch-size servings
Serving Size: ⅙ of pie
Preparation Time:
  20 minutes

Nutritional Analysis
per serving

Calories	307
Protein	19 g
Carbohydrate	23.9 g
Fiber	1.8 g
Sugar	3.3 g
Fat	14.8 g
Cholesterol	87.7 mg
Saturated Fat	4.3 g
Mono Fat	6.3 g
Poly Fat	2.8 g
Folate	70 Ug
Vitamin C	5 mg
Sodium	866 mg
Potassium	273 mg
Iron	3 mg
Calcium	246 mg

Spaghetti Squash with Cream Cheese Sauce

1	spaghetti squash 3½ lbs. (1.75 kg)	1
½ cup	light cream cheese	125 mL
½ cup	1% milk	125 mL
2 tbsp.	Parmesan cheese	25 mL
4 slices	bacon, diced, cooked crisp	4
	fresh ground pepper	

- Place the squash on a microwavable dish, pierce 6 times with the point of a knife.
- Microwave on High 4 minutes; turn over and cook 4 minutes more. Let stand 10 minutes.
- Halve squash lengthwise and remove seeds.
- Cover each half and cook 4 minutes each on High, or until a fork can easily remove strands of squash.
- Scrape squash well with fork to remove all strands. Place strands in a serving bowl; cover to keep hot.
- To prepare sauce, in a microwavable bowl, combine cream cheese and milk.
- Heat on High for 1½ minutes. Stir.
- Heat on Medium for another 1½ minutes, or until smooth and hot.
- Stir in Parmesan cheese. Pour over spaghetti squash and lightly toss.
- Sprinkle with diced bacon and freshly ground pepper.

Serve with a whole-grain baguette.

Variations: Try your favorite zesty tomato herb pasta sauce or tomato-meat sauce on spaghetti squash cooked as above.

Yield: 4 servings
Serving Size:
 1 cup (250 mL)
Preparation Time:
 30 minutes

Nutritional Analysis
per serving

Calories	201
Protein	8.6 g
Carbohydrate	19.3 g
Fiber	5 g
Sugar	10.2 g
Fat	10.3 g
Cholesterol	23.6 mg
Saturated Fat	5.5 g
Mono Fat	1.9 g
Poly Fat	.9 g
Folate	57 Ug
Vitamin C	18 mg
Sodium	315 mg
Potassium	920 mg
Iron	1 mg
Calcium	138 mg

Black Bean Stir-fry

6 cups	combined mixed vegetables, e.g., sliced carrot, baby corn, green and red pepper, broccoli, cauliflower, sugar peas and onion	1.5 L
1 tbsp.	canola oil	15 mL
1 lb.	fresh Peking-style thick noodles*	500 g
1 cup	vegetable stock, page 42	250 mL
1 cup	cooked black beans	250 mL
2	large garlic cloves, crushed	2
2 tsp.	cornstarch	10 mL
¾ cup	cold water	175 mL
1 tbsp.	granulated sugar	15 mL
2 tbsp.	black bean sauce	25 mL
½ tsp.	sesame oil	2 mL
½ tsp.	chili hot sauce OR crushed chili flakes	2 mL
¼ tsp.	ground ginger	1 mL

- In a wok or large frying pan, over medium-high heat, stir-fry vegetables in oil for 4 minutes.
- Reduce heat to medium-low, add noodles, stock and beans. Stir; cover and cook for 5 minutes.
- In a bowl, combine garlic, cornstarch, cold water, sugar, black bean sauce, sesame oil, chili sauce and ginger. Add to wok. Increase heat to medium. Cook for 2 to 3 minutes, until sauce is thickened.

* These noodles are available in large supermarkets or Oriental groceries.

Variations: Substitute linguine or fettuccine for Peking-style noodles, if you prefer. This delicious vegetarian dish can also be adapted to include shrimp or thinly sliced sirloin steak. See Mandarin Beef Stir-Fry Method on page 180.

Pictured on the front cover.

Yield: 4 servings
Serving Size: 2 cups (500 mL)
Preparation Time: 18 minutes

Nutritional Analysis
per serving

Calories	716
Protein	28.4 g
Carbohydrate	133.3 g
Fiber	19.3 g
Sugar	19.9 g
Fat	9.8 g
Cholesterol	107.7 mg
Saturated Fat	1.5 g
Mono Fat	1.7 g
Poly Fat	2.9 g
Folate	149 Ug
Vitamin C	9 mg
Sodium	412 mg
Potassium	894 mg
Iron	8 mg
Calcium	120 mg

Pesto Penne

The fresh flavor of pesto makes it a favorite with many. Make a big batch of Pesto when fresh basil is available and freeze it in ice cube trays. Store the pesto cubes in freezer bags and use as needed.

2½ cups	penne pasta	625 mL

Pesto

¼ cup	chopped fresh basil	50 mL
¼ cup	chopped fresh parsley	50 mL
¼ cup	chopped green onion	50 mL
¼ cup	grated Parmesan cheese	50 mL
2 tbsp.	toasted pine nuts*	25 mL
1	garlic clove, chopped	1
3 tbsp.	olive oil	45 mL
½ tsp.	salt	2 mL
	freshly ground pepper	

- Cook penne as per package directions. Drain and keep warm.
- In a food processor, combine basil, parsley, green onion, Parmesan, pine nuts, garlic, olive oil, salt and pepper. Process for 6 seconds, or until ingredients are finely chopped.
- Spoon pesto over warm penne, toss to coat. Serve immediately.

* Pine nuts should be stored in an airtight container in the refrigerator or freezer. Almonds may be substituted, but the pine nut flavor is superior for pesto.

Yield: 4 servings

Serving Size: 1 cup (250 mL)

Preparation time: 20 minutes

Nutritional Analysis
per serving

Calories	466
Protein	14.6 g
Carbohydrate	66.7 g
Fiber	2.6 g
Sugar	3.1 g
Fat	15.6 g
Cholesterol	3.9 mg
Saturated Fat	2.9 g
Mono Fat	9 g
Poly Fat	2.5 g
Folate	27 Ug
Vitamin C	6 mg
Sodium	393 mg
Potassium	214 mg
Iron	5 mg
Calcium	96 mg

Broccoli, Mushrooms and Tortellini in Creamy Garlic Sauce

3½ cups	fresh OR frozen chicken tortellini	825 mL
2 cups	bite-sized broccoli florets	500 mL

Creamy Garlic Sauce

1 tsp.	olive oil	5 mL
6	extra-large mushrooms, quartered	6
¾ cup	1% milk	175 mL
4 oz.	light cream cheese	125 g
2	garlic cloves, crushed	2
½ tsp.	salt	2 mL
	freshly ground pepper to taste	
2 tbsp.	Parmesan cheese	25 mL

- In a large pot or Dutch oven, bring 10 cups (2.5 L) of water to a boil.
- Add tortellini; cook, uncovered, for 10 minutes.
- Add broccoli florets and cook for 5 minutes.
- Meanwhile, in a large saucepan, heat olive oil over medium to medium-low heat. Add mushrooms. Cook for 2 minutes, stirring constantly.
- Reduce heat to low, add milk, cream cheese and garlic. Cook, stirring and breaking up cream cheese, until a smooth sauce forms.
- Add salt and pepper.
- Drain tortellini and broccoli.
- Toss tortellini and broccoli in cream sauce.
- Sprinkle with Parmesan cheese and toss again. Serve immediately.

Variation: Slivered red pepper, sautéed with the mushrooms, gives beautiful color and added flavor.

Pasta
Spicy Sausage Pasta, page 137

Yield: 4 servings
Serving size: 1¼ cups (300 mL)
Preparation time: 35 minutes

Nutritional Analysis
per serving

Calories	348
Protein	17.4 g
Carbohydrate	42.2 g
Fiber	9.4 g
Sugar	5.2 g
Fat	12.4 g
Cholesterol	52.1 mg
Saturated Fat	7.1 g
Mono Fat	3 g
Poly Fat	.3 g
Folate	56 Ug
Vitamin C	60 mg
Sodium	943 mg
Potassium	468 mg
Iron	2 mg
Calcium	218 mg

Spaghetti and Italian Vegetables

½ lb.	spaghetti	250 g
4 cups	chopped mixed Italian vegetables*	1 L
3 tbsp.	butter	45 mL
2 cups	chopped Roma tomatoes	500 mL
¼ tsp.	red chili flakes	1 mL
1	garlic clove, crushed	1
½ cup	chicken stock, page 43	125 mL
2 tsp.	Italian blend seasoning	10 mL
1 tsp.	granulated sugar	5 mL
¼ cup	Parmesan cheese	50 mL

- Cook spaghetti as per package directions. Drain well.
- Cook vegetables in microwave-safe bowl on High for 9 minutes, or until cooked tender-crisp, stirring every 3 minutes.
- In a large saucepan or Dutch oven, over medium to medium-low heat, melt butter and sauté Roma tomatoes for 5 minutes.
- Add chili flakes, chicken stock, sugar and Italian seasoning.
- Add spaghetti and toss with 2 forks.
- Sprinkle with Parmesan cheese and toss again.

* For a fresh vegetable mixture, use sliced zucchini, broccoli, cauliflower, mushrooms, red and/or green peppers, spinach, tomatoes, etc. Frozen vegetables were used for convenience and for consistency in doing the nutritional analysis. Use fresh or frozen vegetables as you prefer.

Yield: 4 servings

Serving Size: 2 cups
(500 mL) 4 servings
Preparation Time:
25 minutes

Nutritional Analysis

per serving

Calories	301
Protein	10.7 g
Carbohydrate	49.4 g
Fiber	7 g
Sugar	8.9 g
Fat	8.2 g
Cholesterol	19 mg
Saturated Fat	4.6 g
Mono Fat	2.2 g
Poly Fat	.7 g
Folate	40 Ug
Vitamin C	16 mg
Sodium	600 mg
Potassium	427 mg
Iron	3 mg
Calcium	90 mg

Wagon Wheels and Cheese Sauce

Kids love pasta and they have their favorite pasta shapes, use this simple and tasty cheese sauce with shells, spirals, etc.

2 cups	wagon wheel pasta	500 mL

Cheese Sauce

2 tbsp.	butter	25 mL
2 tbsp.	all-purpose flour	25 mL
1 cup	1% milk	250 mL
1 tsp.	salt	5 mL
½ tsp.	granulated sugar	2 mL
1 cup	shredded old Cheddar cheese	250 mL
2 tbsp.	sour cream	25 mL
	freshly ground pepper to taste	

- Cook pasta as per package directions.
- To prepare sauce, melt butter in a small saucepan over medium heat.
- Stir in flour; mix well.
- Slowly add milk, stirring constantly.
- Cook until sauce thickens.
- Reduce heat to low, add salt, sugar and Cheddar. Stir until cheese is melted.
- Stir in sour cream and pepper to taste.
- Drain pasta, put into a serving bowl and pour sauce over. Mix well.

Nutrition Tips:

Why do I get cramps if I exercise after I eat?
You may feel discomfort because the blood that would normally go to the digestive tract after eating is busy with the working muscles. This causes normal digestion to be hampered.

Yield: 4 servings
Serving Size: 1 cup
  (250 mL)
Preparation Time:
  15 minutes

Nutritional Analysis
per serving

Calories	321
Protein	13.1 g
Carbohydrate	26.9 g
Fiber	1.5 g
Sugar	4.8 g
Fat	17.9 g
Cholesterol	51.6 mg
Saturated Fat	11 g
Mono Fat	5 g
Poly Fat	.8 g
Folate	15 Ug
Vitamin C	1 mg
Sodium	854 mg
Potassium	161 mg
Iron	2 mg
Calcium	295 mg

Cottage Cheese and Noodles

8 oz.	broad noodles (about 5 cups [1.25 L] OR 4 cups [1 L]) cooked	250 g
1	large onion, chopped	1
¼ cup	butter OR margarine	50 mL
16 oz.	dry curd cottage cheese	500 g
2	eggs	2
½ cup	1% milk	125 mL
1 tsp.	salt	5 mL
¼ tsp.	black pepper	1 mL
	paprika	

- Cook noodles as per package directions, but use only ½ tsp. (2 mL) salt, in the boiling water. Drain.
- Preheat oven to 350°F (180°C).
- In a medium frying pan, over medium heat, sauté onions in butter until browned, about 7 minutes.
- In a lightly greased 8-cup (2 L) casserole, combine noodles, cottage cheese and fried onions.
- In a small bowl, whisk together eggs, milk, salt and pepper.
- Pour egg mixture over noodles; stir well to coat.
- Bake, covered, for 30 minutes, stirring once after 15 minutes.
- Sprinkle with paprika before serving.

Variation: Try 1 tsp. (5 mL) poppy seed or caraway seeds as a garnish.

Yield: 6 servings
Serving Size:
  1¼ cups (300 mL)
Preparation Time:
  20 minutes

Nutritional Analysis
per serving

Calories	322
Protein	21.3 g
Carbohydrate	31.4 g
Fiber	1.7 g
Sugar	2.9 g
Fat	11.9 g
Cholesterol	133.5 mg
Saturated Fat	6.2 g
Mono Fat	3.6 g
Poly Fat	1 g
Folate	33 Ug
Vitamin C	2 mg
Sodium	519 mg
Potassium	152 mg
Iron	2 mg
Calcium	78 mg

Basic Tomato Sauce

1 cup	chopped onion	250 mL
2	celery stalks, chopped	2
½ cup	chopped green pepper	125 mL
1 tbsp.	olive oil	15 mL
1	garlic clove, minced	1
28 oz.	can diced tomatoes	796 mL
5½ oz.	can tomato paste	156 mL
1½ cups	water	375 mL
2 tbsp.	Italian herb seasoning*	25 mL
1 tbsp.	granulated sugar	15 mL

- In a large saucepan, over medium to medium-low heat, sauté onion, celery and green pepper in olive oil for 5 minutes.
- Add garlic, tomatoes, tomato paste, water, Italian seasoning and sugar. Stir.
- Bring to a boil, reduce heat to a simmer and simmer 30 minutes, stirring occasionally.
- Remove from heat, cool 15 minutes, stirring occasionally.
- Purée in a blender or food processor until smooth.

Variations: Add crushed red chili flakes for a spicier sauce. If you prefer a chunky sauce, do not purée. For **Basic Tomato and Meat Sauce**, brown 1 lb. (500 g) lean ground beef, drain off fat; add onions, celery and green peppers. Add the garlic, etc. and proceed as above. Add salt and pepper to taste. Do NOT purée

* Fresh herbs in season add wonderful flavor. To make your own Italian herb seasoning combine oregano, basil, thyme, rosemary, sage, savory, marjoram.

**Yield:
Approximately
8 servings
(6 cups [1.5 L]
of sauce)**
Serving Size: ¾ cup
(175 mL)

Nutritional Analysis
per serving

Calories	80
Protein	2.6 g
Carbohydrate	18.1 g
Fiber	2.5 g
Sugar	6.9 g
Fat	1.9 g
Cholesterol	0 mg
Saturated Fat	.3 g
Mono Fat	1.3 g
Poly Fat	.2 g
Folate	15 Ug
Vitamin C	29 mg
Sodium	1116 mg
Potassium	433 mg
Iron	1 mg
Calcium	47 mg

Stir-Fry Noodles and Crab

4.5 oz.	rice stick noodles	126 g
2 cups	chopped mixed Chinese vegetables*	500 mL
1 tsp.	canola oil	5 mL
¼ cup	water	50 mL
¾ cup	vegetable cocktail juice	175 mL
3 tbsp.	rice wine vinegar	45 mL
2 tbsp.	teriyaki sauce	25 mL
2 tbsp.	granulated sugar	25 mL
1-2	garlic cloves, minced	1-2
1 tsp.	sesame oil	5 mL
¼ tsp.	chili flakes	1 mL
1 lb.	crab OR pollock flakes	500 g
½ cup	julienned English cucumber	125 mL
2 tbsp.	chopped cilantro	25 mL
1	green onion, sliced	1
	chopped peanuts to garnish	

- In a large saucepan, cook rice noodles in boiling water for 3-5 minutes. Drain. Rinse in cold water.
- In a large frying pan or wok over medium-high heat, heat canola oil. Add mixed Chinese vegetables; cook and stir constantly for 3 minutes.
- Turn heat to low, add water. Cover and steam for 1½ minutes.
- Remove vegetables from heat; put into a 10-cup (2.5 L) salad bowl. Let cool.
- To prepare dressing, in a small bowl, combine vegetable cocktail juice, rice vinegar, teriyaki sauce, sugar, garlic, sesame oil and chili flakes.
- Using 2 forks, toss noodles with vegetables.
- Add crab, cucumber, cilantro and dressing.
- Sprinkle with onions and peanuts.

Serve as a main course salad or as part of a Chinese dinner.

* Use a combination of snow peas, bok choy, broccoli, red and/or green peppers, green onions, carrots, etc. For nutritional analysis purposes, 12 oz. (350 g) of frozen prepared mixed Chinese vegetables was used.

Yield: 4 servings
Serving Size: 2 cups
(500 mL)
Preparation Time:
30 minutes

Nutritional Analysis
per serving

Calories	222
Protein	15.6 g
Carbohydrate	31.5 g
Fiber	1.9 g
Sugar	7 g
Fat	4 g
Cholesterol	22.7 mg
Saturated Fat	.6 g
Mono Fat	.7 g
Poly Fat	1.6 g
Folate	16 Ug
Vitamin C	28 mg
Sodium	1473 mg
Potassium	248 mg
Iron	2 mg
Calcium	32 mg

Prawn and Asparagus Fettuccine

Lemon Garlic Dressing

¼ cup	olive oil	50 mL
¼ cup	freshly squeezed lemon juice	50 mL
1	garlic clove, crushed	1
½ tsp.	salt	2 mL
12 oz.	pkg. fresh fettuccine	250 g
½ lb.	asparagus cut into 2" (5 cm) lengths	250 g
1 lb.	cooked black tiger prawns (31-38 prawns)	500 g
¼ cup	Parmesan cheese	50 mL
	freshly ground pepper to taste	
¼ cup	chopped parsley	50 mL

- In a small bowl, whisk together olive oil, lemon juice, garlic and salt. Set aside.
- Cook fettuccine in boiling water for 3 to 5 minutes. Drain and keep warm.
- Steam asparagus to tender-crisp, about 4 minutes.
- Reheat shrimp in boiling water for 1 minute. Drain.
- In a large, preheated pasta bowl, toss fettuccine, asparagus and prawns with 2 forks.
- Drizzle dressing over pasta. Sprinkle with Parmesan.
- Grind pepper over top and toss.
- Sprinkle with parsley and serve.

Yield: 4 servings
Serving Size: 2 cups
(500 mL)
Preparation Time:
25 minutes

Nutritional Analysis
per serving

Calories	502
Protein	33.5 g
Carbohydrate	51.4 g
Fiber	2.3 g
Sugar	1.5 g
Fat	19.1 g
Cholesterol	311.4 mg
Saturated Fat	3.8 g
Mono Fat	10.7 g
Poly Fat	2.7 g
Folate	85 Ug
Vitamin C	18 mg
Sodium	542 mg
Potassium	344 mg
Iron	5 mg
Calcium	176 mg

Tuna Fusilli Bake

2½ cups	fusilli pasta	625 mL
6 oz.	can water-packed tuna, drained	170 g
1 tbsp.	canola oil	15 mL
½ cup	chopped onion	125 mL
2	celery stalks, sliced	2
1 cup	chopped mushrooms	250 mL
2	garlic cloves, crushed	2
4 tsp.	cornstarch	20 mL
1½ cups	1% milk	375 mL
¼ cup	grated Cheddar cheese	50 mL
2 tbsp.	ketchup	25 mL
1 tsp.	salt	5 mL
¼ tsp.	lemon pepper	1 mL
½ cup	crushed, cheese-flavored taco chips	125 mL

- Preheat oven to 350°F (180°C).
- Cook pasta as per package directions. Drain.
- Spray an 8-cup (2 L) casserole with nonstick cooking spray. Add cooked, drained pasta and drained tuna. Stir to break up tuna chunks.
- In a medium saucepan, over medium heat, add the oil and onion. Cook, stirring occasionally, for 3 minutes.
- Add celery, mushrooms and garlic. Stir.
- Whisk together cornstarch and milk. Pour into saucepan. Cook, stirring constantly, until it starts to thicken. Reduce heat to medium low.
- Add cheese, ketchup, salt and lemon pepper. Stir until cheese melts.
- Pour sauce mixture over pasta and tuna. Mix well.
- Sprinkle with crushed taco chips.
- Bake 20 to 25 minutes, or until heated through.

Yield: 6 servings
Serving Size: 1⅓ cups (325 mL)
Preparation Time: 25 minutes

Nutritional Analysis
per serving

Calories	359
Protein	18.9 g
Carbohydrate	54.6 g
Fiber	2.2 g
Sugar	6.3 g
Fat	6.9 g
Cholesterol	16.2 mg
Saturated Fat	2 g
Mono Fat	.8 g
Poly Fat	1.3 g
Folate	25 Ug
Vitamin C	4 mg
Sodium	670 mg
Potassium	392 mg
Iron	3 mg
Calcium	134 mg

Creamy Tuna and Peas on Seashells

2 cups	small seashell pasta	500 mL
2 tbsp.	butter	25 mL
2 tbsp.	all-purpose flour	25 mL
1 cup	1% milk	250 mL
½ tsp.	salt	2 mL
⅛ tsp.	black pepper	0.5 mL
1 cup	frozen peas	250 mL
6 oz.	can flaked tuna in water*	170 g
1 tbsp.	chopped parsley	15 mL

- Cook seashell pasta as per package directions. Drain and keep warm.
- In a saucepan, over medium heat, melt butter. Stir in flour and mix well.
- Slowly add milk, stirring constantly.
- Add salt and pepper. Cook until thick. Reduce heat to medium-low.
- Add peas and tuna with liquid from can. Cook for 10 minutes.
- Stir in parsley. Serve over seashell pasta.

* For **Creamy Crab and Peas on Seashells**, substitute flaked crab for tuna if you prefer.

Yield: 4 servings
Serving Size:
  1 cup (250 mL) pasta,
  ½ cup (125 mL) sauce
Preparation Time:
  20 minutes

Nutritional Analysis
per serving

Calories	250
Protein	17.1 g
Carbohydrate	25.7 g
Fiber	3 g
Sugar	7 g
Fat	8.1 g
Cholesterol	36.7 mg
Saturated Fat	4.5 g
Mono Fat	2.3 g
Poly Fat	.8 g
Folate	30 Ug
Vitamin C	6 mg
Sodium	579 mg
Potassium	312 mg
Iron	2 mg
Calcium	95 mg

Nutrition Tips:

The best time to replenish your carbohydrate stores is within 15 minutes of completing exercise. Drink a fruit juice, keep a bagel in your gym bag, eat an apple, even munch on licorice!

Stroganoff Meatballs on Spaghetti

These creamy meatballs are also good with
Cottage Cheese and Noodles, page 127.

1 lb.	lean ground beef	500 g
½ cup	quick-cooking oatmeal	125 mL
1	egg	1
1	carrot, grated	1
2 tbsp.	grated onion	25 mL
½ tsp.	salt	2 mL
1 cup	beef stock, page 44	250 mL
2 tbsp.	all-purpose flour	25 mL
⅓ cup	cold water	75 mL
⅓ cup	sour cream	75 mL
	chopped fresh OR dried parsley	
	spaghetti, for 6, 1½ lbs. (750 g)	

- In a large bowl, combine beef, oatmeal, egg, carrot, onion and salt. Mix well.
- Scoop ⅛ cup (25 mL) of the beef mixture and form into meatball. Make 24 meatballs.
- Heat a nonstick frying pan over medium to medium-low heat.
- Cook meatballs until browned on all sides, about 10 minutes. Turn heat to low or medium-low; cover and cook another 10 minutes, until center of meatballs is no longer pink.
- Remove meatballs to a 6-cup (1.5 L) casserole. Keep warm in oven.
- Drain drippings from the frying pan. Return the pan to the heat. Pour stock into the pan, scraping up bits from the bottom.
- In a small bowl, combine flour and cold water. Stir until smooth. Slowly pour flour mixture into stock in frying pan, stirring constantly.
- Cook until it bubbles and is thickened.
- Remove from heat; add sour cream; stir well.
- Pour sauce over meatballs; stir and sprinkle with parsley.

Serve with spaghetti.

Yield: 6 servings
Serving size: 4 meatballs
Preparation Time: 14 minutes

Nutritional Analysis
per serving

Calories	300
Protein	24.3 g
Carbohydrate	10.8 g
Fiber	1 g
Sugar	1 g
Fat	17.2 g
Cholesterol	112.9 mg
Saturated Fat	7.1 g
Mono Fat	7.1 g
Poly Fat	1 g
Folate	20 Ug
Vitamin C	2 mg
Sodium	416 mg
Potassium	387 mg
Iron	3 mg
Calcium	38 mg

Veal Lasagne with Béchamel Sauce

1 tbsp.	olive oil	15 mL
½ lb.	ground veal	250 g
½	onion, minced	½
½	green pepper, minced	½
2	celery stalks, minced	2
1	carrot, minced	1
2	garlic cloves, minced	2
19 oz.	can crushed tomatoes	540 mL
1 tsp.	crushed red chili flakes	5 mL
1 tsp.	crushed oregano	5 mL
1 tsp.	crushed basil	5 mL
¼ tsp.	crushed rosemary	1 mL
½ cup	water	125 mL
10 oz.	frozen chopped spinach, thawed, drained	300 g
1 tbsp.	brown sugar	15 mL
2 tsp.	salt	10 mL
6-8	cooked lasagne noodles, drained	6-8
¼ cup	freshly grated Parmesan cheese	50 mL

Béchamel Sauce

¼ cup	butter	50 mL
¼ cup	all-purpose flour	50 mL
½ cup	chicken stock, page 43	125 mL
1½ cups	2% milk	375 mL
2 tbsp.	white wine (optional)	25 mL
¼ tsp.	salt	1 mL
¼ tsp.	nutmeg	1 mL

- In a large saucepan, heat oil over medium heat.
- Add veal, breaking up with a spoon.
- Add onion, green pepper, celery, carrot, garlic and tomatoes, stirring occasionally.
- Cook until meat is brown, no pink is showing.
- Reduce heat to medium low, cook for 15 minutes. Remove from heat.

Veal Lasagne with Béchamel Sauce

continued

- Add chili flakes, oregano, basil, rosemary, water, chopped spinach, sugar and salt. Stir well.
- Return to heat and simmer slowly for 30 minutes.
- To prepare Béchamel Sauce, in a medium saucepan melt butter over medium heat. Add flour; stir well. Slowly add chicken stock and milk, stirring constantly until thickened. Add white wine, salt and nutmeg. Stir and remove from heat.
- Preheat oven to 350°F (180°C).
- Spread 1 cup (250 mL) meat sauce on the bottom of a 9 x 13" (22 x 34 cm) baking dish that has been sprayed with nonstick cooking spray.
- Lay 3 to 4 lasagne noodles on the sauce. Spoon half the remaining meat sauce over, then another layer of noodles then meat sauce.
- Top with 1½ cups (375 mL) Béchamel Sauce. Smooth over.
- Sprinkle with Parmesan cheese.
- Bake for 40 to 45 minutes, until hot and bubbly and the top is browning.

Serve with Italian bread and Romaine and Pear Salad with Blue Cheese Dressing, page 48.

Variations: For **Beef Lasagne** or **Chicken Lasagne**, substitute ground beef or chicken for the veal.

Yield: 6 servings
Serving Size: 1 square,
4 x 4" (10 x 10 cm)
Preparation Time:
45 minutes

Nutritional Analysis

per serving

Calories	455
Protein	19.2 g
Carbohydrate	58.8 g
Fiber	4.9 g
Sugar	12.6 g
Fat	15.7 g
Cholesterol	52.2 mg
Saturated Fat	7.6 g
Mono Fat	5.3 g
Poly Fat	1.3 g
Folate	59 Ug
Vitamin C	23 mg
Sodium	1374 mg
Potassium	439 mg
Iron	4 mg
Calcium	238 mg

Beef and Tomato Macaroni Bake

2 cups	uncooked macaroni	500 mL
1 lb.	lean ground beef	500 g
1	small onion, finely chopped	1
2	garlic cloves, minced	2
28 oz.	can tomatoes with herbs	796 mL
¼ cup	tomato paste	50 mL
12 oz.	light quark	340 g
1 tsp.	granulated sugar	5 mL
½ tsp.	salt	2 mL
¼ tsp.	black pepper	1 mL
⅛ tsp.	cinnamon	0.5 mL
1	egg	1
½ cup	1% milk	125 mL
¼ cup	light Parmesan cheese	50 mL
¼ tsp.	salt	1 mL
1 cup	grated partly skimmed mozzarella cheese	250 mL

- Preheat oven to 350°F (180°C).
- Cook macaroni as per package directions but use only ½ tsp. (2 mL) of salt in the water. Drain.
- In a large frying pan, brown beef, onion and garlic for 10 minutes, or until no pink shows.
- While the beef is browning, mix tomatoes, tomato paste, ½ cup (125 mL) quark, sugar, salt, pepper and cinnamon in blender. Blend until smooth and creamy.
- Stir into cooked beef along with the macaroni. Heat just until it starts to bubble.
- Spray a 9 x 13" (22 x 34 cm) baking pan with nonstick cooking spray.
- Spoon the beef mixture into the baking pan. Rinse blender and add remaining quark, egg, milk, Parmesan and salt. Blend well. Pour quark mixture evenly over hamburger mixture. Sprinkle with mozzarella.
- Bake for 45 minutes, or until browned on top.

Yield: 8 servings
Serving Size:
1, 4½ x 3" piece
(11 x 7.5 cm)
Preparation Time:
30 minutes

Nutritional Analysis
per serving

Calories	340
Protein	28.3 g
Carbohydrate	29.7 g
Fiber	2 g
Sugar	6.3 g
Fat	11.1 g
Cholesterol	78.2 mg
Saturated Fat	4.7 g
Mono Fat	4.3 g
Poly Fat	6 g
Folate	16 Ug
Vitamin C	13 mg
Sodium	564 mg
Potassium	303 mg
Iron	3 mg
Calcium	178 mg

Spicy Sausage Pasta

¾ lb.	mild OR hot Italian sausage (about 3)	350 g
2 tsp.	olive oil	10 mL
1	large onion, chopped	1
1	green pepper, diced	1
1 cup	sliced fresh mushrooms	250 mL
1	small zucchini, halved lengthwise, and cut into ¼" (6 mm) crosswise slices	1
2	garlic cloves, crushed	2
3 cups	Basic Tomato sauce*, page 128	750 mL
2 tbsp.	brown sugar	25 mL
4 tsp.	Worcestershire sauce	20 mL
½ tsp.	crushed oregano	2 mL
½ tsp.	dried basil	2 mL

- In a large frying pan, over medium heat, brown sausages in olive oil. When fully cooked, remove sausages from pan and drain off all fat except for 1 tbsp. (15 mL)
- Add onions to the frying pan. Cook until soft, for 2 minutes.
- Cut sausages into ¼" (6 mm) slices and add to onions.
- Add green pepper, mushrooms, zucchini, garlic, pasta sauce, brown sugar, Worcestershire sauce, oregano and basil.
- Bring to a simmer and cook for 30 minutes, stirring frequently.

Serve with your favorite pasta.

Note: An average pasta portion is ¼ pound (125 g), so use 2 pounds (1 kg) for this amount of sauce.

* You may substitute a commercial spicy pasta sauce when you're in a hurry.

Pictured on page 123.

Yield: 8 servings
Freezes well
Serving Size: ¾ cup (175 mL)
Preparation Time: 25 minutes

Nutritional Analysis
per serving

Calories	280
Protein	11 g
Carbohydrate	22.9 g
Fiber	4.1 g
Sugar	4.8 g
Fat	16.6 g
Cholesterol	33.2 mg
Saturated Fat	4.7 g
Mono Fat	8.2 g
Poly Fat	2.8 g
Folate	34 Ug
Vitamin C	27 mg
Sodium	883 mg
Potassium	647 mg
Iron	2 mg
Calcium	54 mg

Spaghetti and Sausage Pie

*A great plan-ahead meal, eat one hot,
and freeze the other to enjoy later.*

10½ oz.	package spaghetti	300 g
1 tbsp.	olive oil	15 mL
¼ cup	Parmesan cheese	50 mL
1	egg, lightly beaten	1
2¾ cups	Basic Tomato Sauce, page 128	675 mL
½ cup	diced onion	125 mL
1 cup	thinly sliced ham sausage	250 mL
2 cups	sliced mushrooms	500 mL
2 cups	shredded partly skimmed mozzarella	500 mL
1	green pepper, diced	1
½ tsp.	crushed oregano	2 mL
½ tsp.	crushed basil	2 mL
½ tsp.	crushed chili flakes	2 mL

- Cook spaghetti as per package instructions.
- Drain spaghetti and transfer to a bowl; toss with olive oil; cool.
- Toss with Parmesan cheese and egg.
- Preheat oven to 375°F (190°C).
- Evenly divide spaghetti between 2, 9" (22 cm) deep pie plates sprayed with nonstick cooking spray. Press over bottom and sides to form a shell.
- Spoon equal amounts of tomato sauce over each, smoothing out with a spoon.
- Divide onion, sausage and mushrooms between the pies.
- Sprinkle each with mozzarella cheese and green pepper. Then sprinkle each with a ¼ tsp. (1 mL) of the oregano, basil and chili flakes.
- Bake for 30 minutes.

Variation: Sauté spicy Italian sausage and substitute for the ham sausage.

**Yield: 2 pies,
6 servings each**
Serving Size: 1 slice
Preparation Time:
40 minutes.

Nutritional Analysis
per serving

Calories	227
Protein	14.1 g
Carbohydrate	26.7 g
Fiber	1.8 g
Sugar	3.6 g
Fat	7.9 g
Cholesterol	37.1 mg
Saturated Fat	3.2 g
Mono Fat	2.3 g
Poly Fat	.6 g
Folate	17 Ug
Vitamin C	15 mg
Sodium	707 mg
Potassium	312 mg
Iron	2 mg
Calcium	216 mg

FISH & MEAT DISHES

HEALTHY EATING FOR HEALTHY LIFESTYLES

Greek Baked Fish

This easy fish dish tastes as great as it looks. The tomato and feta combination is hard to beat.

2 lbs.	haddock fillet, OR other fish fillet	1 kg
2 tbsp.	lemon juice	25 mL
½ tsp.	seasoning salt	2 mL
2	tomatoes, diced	2
3	garlic cloves, minced	3
2 tsp.	crushed oregano	10 mL
2 tsp.	olive oil	10 mL
½ cup	crumbed feta cheese	125 mL

- Preheat oven to 350°F (180°C).
- Lightly grease a 9 x 13" (22 x 34 cm) pan.
- Place fillets in pan and sprinkle with lemon juice and seasoning salt.
- Sprinkle with tomatoes, garlic and oregano.
- Drizzle olive oil over the tomato topping.
- Top with crumbled feta.
- Bake for 35 minutes, or until the fish flakes with a fork.

Nutrition Tips:

Losses of 2 to 3 percent of body weight due to sweating can reduce aerobic ability by more than 10 percent. This would be equivalent to 3 pounds (1.5 k) on a 160-pound (72.5 k) person.

Fish

Greek Baked Fish, page 140

Crispy Potato Wedges, page 116

Yield: 4 servings
Serving Size: ¼ of recipe
Preparation Time: 12 minutes

Nutritional Analysis
per serving

Calories	302
Protein	43.8 g
Carbohydrate	6.1 g
Fiber	1.1 g
Sugar	1.9 g
Fat	10.8 g
Cholesterol	145.6 mg
Saturated Fat	5.4 g
Mono Fat	3.4 g
Poly Fat	1 g
Folate	44 Ug
Vitamin C	16 mg
Sodium	669 mg
Potassium	821 mg
Iron	3 mg
Calcium	243 mg

Stuffed Rainbow Trout

2 lb.	rainbow trout, head and tail removed	1 kg
1½ cups	cooked brown and wild rice	375 mL
¼ cup	minced carrot	50 mL
¼ cup	minced celery	50 mL
	freshly ground pepper	
1 tsp.	soft butter	5 mL
½ tsp.	seasoning salt	2 mL
1 tsp.	mixed herb and spice seasoning (salt free)	5 mL
1	lemon, cut in half lengthwise	1

- Preheat oven to 350°F (180°C).
- Lay fish on a sheet of foil wrap 24" (60 cm) long.
- With a sharp knife, open cavity to the tail end.
- In a small bowl, combine rice, carrot, celery and pepper.
- Wipe inside of fish dry with paper towel.
- With fingers, spread butter on inside of fish.
- Sprinkle cavity lightly with seasoning salt and the herb and spice seasoning.
- Cut ½ of the lemon into 8 slices crosswise. Reserve the other half for serving.
- Lay the lemon slices against the inside flesh along both sides.
- Hold the fish so the cavity is facing up and the backbone is on the counter. Stuff with rice mixture. Press lightly to pack.
- Carefully lay fish on its side. Fold foil to form a sealed packet. Place on a baking sheet.
- Bake for 45 minutes. Remove fish from oven and let sit for 10 minutes.
- Remove fish from foil. Place on a serving plate.
- Cut the reserved lemon into 4 pieces and arrange beside the fish.

Serve with Baby Greens with Fresh Lemon Dressing, page 45.

Yield: 4 servings

Serving Size: ¼ fish plus ½ cup (125 mL) dressing

Preparation Time: 15 minutes

Nutritional Analysis

per serving

Calories	449
Protein	50.2 g
Carbohydrate	38.7 g
Fiber	5.3 g
Sugar	1.2 g
Fat	9.7 g
Cholesterol	127 mg
Saturated Fat	2.1 g
Mono Fat	2.6 g
Poly Fat	2.7 g
Folate	20 Ug
Vitamin C	28 mg
Sodium	523 mg
Potassium	1487 mg
Iron	5 mg
Calcium	192 mg

Salmon Loaf

2 x 7¾ oz.	cans pink salmon	2 x 220 mL
2 tbsp.	ketchup	25 mL
1 tbsp.	lemon juice	15 mL
2	eggs, beaten	2
1 cup	rolled oats	250 mL
1 cup	grated Cheddar cheese	250 mL
1	green onion, sliced	1
1	celery stalk, diced	1
1	large carrot, shredded	1
½ tsp.	Mrs. Dash original seasoning	2 mL
¼ tsp.	lemon pepper	1 mL
2 cups	Mushroom Soup*, page 41	500 mL

- Preheat oven to 350°F (180°C).
- In a large bowl, place salmon and the juice. Mash skin and bones with a fork.
- Add ketchup, lemon juice, eggs, rolled oats, Cheddar cheese, onion, celery, carrot, Mrs. Dash seasoning and lemon pepper. Mix well.
- Spoon mixture into a 3 x 4½ x 8½" (6.5 x 12 x 21 cm) loaf pan.
- Bake 40 minutes, until edges are browned and center is firm.
- Bring Mushroom Sauce to a simmer over medium heat, stirring often so sauce doesn't scorch.
- Turn salmon loaf onto a heated platter. Spoon over half the sauce. Serve the remainder of the sauce at serving time.

Serve with cottage cheese and noodles or brown and wild rice.

* For convenience, you may substitute a 10 oz. (284 mL) can of low-fat mushroom soup, ¾ cup (175 mL) of water and ½ cup (125 mL) thinly sliced mushrooms, simmered gently just to heat, for Mushroom Sauce.

Yield: 4 servings (8, 1" [2.5 cm] slices)
Serving Size: 2, 1" (2.5 cm) slices
Preparation Time: 25 minutes

\Nutritional Analysis
per serving

Calories	367
Protein	27.2 g
Carbohydrate	22.9 g
Fiber	2.3 g
Sugar	5.8 g
Fat	18.6 g
Cholesterol	156.7 mg
Saturated Fat	9 g
Mono Fat	5.6 g
Poly Fat	2.5 g
Folate	46 Ug
Vitamin C	7 mg
Sodium	869 mg
Potassium	636 mg
Iron	2 mg
Calcium	402 mg

Salmon Patties

This old-fashioned salmon dish is fast, easy, nutritious, and a family-tested favorite.

7.5 oz.	can pink salmon, drained	213 g
2 cups	leftover mashed potatoes	500 mL
1	egg, lightly beaten	1
2	green onions, thinly sliced	2
dash	black pepper	dash
⅓ cup	dry bread crumbs	75 mL
2 tbsp.	margarine, divided	25 mL
1 tbsp.	canola oil	15 mL

- In a medium bowl, mash salmon with a fork.
- Add mashed potatoes, egg, green onion and pepper. Mix well. Chill 30 minutes.
- Make salmon mixture into small patties of approximately ¼ cup (50 mL) size. Coat in bread crumbs.
- Heat a heavy nonstick frying pan over medium heat. Add 1 tbsp. (15 mL) margarine and the oil.
- When the margarine is melted, add the salmon patties. Fry 5 minutes, until nicely browned. Turn over, add the other 1 tbsp. (15 mL) margarine. Cook another 5 minutes, or until browned.

Serve with Back-to-Basics Salad, page 46.

Yield: 10 servings

Serving Size: 2 patties
Preparation Time:
   7 minutes,
   chilling time
   30 minutes

Nutritional Analysis
per serving

Calories	118
Protein	5.8 g
Carbohydrate	7.9 g
Fiber	.9 g
Sugar	1.7 g
Fat	7.3 g
Cholesterol	33.8 mg
Saturated Fat	1.4 g
Mono Fat	2.2 g
Poly Fat	2.3 g
Folate	10 Ug
Vitamin C	3 mg
Sodium	287 mg
Potassium	204 mg
Iron	0 mg
Calcium	62 mg

Mexican Roast Chicken with Corn Bread Stuffing

Corn Bread Stuffing*

1 cup	cornmeal	250 mL
¾ cup	all-purpose flour	175 mL
2 tbsp.	granulated sugar	25 mL
½ tsp.	salt	2 mL
1 tbsp.	baking powder	15 mL
1	egg	1
1 cup	1% milk	250 mL
¼ cup	shortening at room temperature	50 mL
3 slices	turkey bacon, diced	3 slices
2 tbsp.	margarine	25 mL
½ cup	chopped onion	125 mL
2	celery stalks, chopped	2
1 tsp.	salt	5 mL
¼ tsp.	black pepper	1 mL
1½ tsp.	poultry seasoning	7 mL
1 cup	chicken stock	250 mL
4 lb.	roasting chicken	2 kg
½	lime	½
1 tsp.	chili powder	5 mL
⅛ tsp.	cumin	0.5 mL
¼ tsp.	salt	1 mL
¼ tsp.	black pepper	1 mL
2 tbsp.	cornstarch	25 mL
1 cup	vegetable cocktail juice	250 mL

- Preheat oven to 425°F (220°C).
- To prepare corn bread, in a medium bowl combine cornmeal, flour, sugar, salt and baking powder.
- Add egg, milk and shortening. Beat with an electric mixer until smooth, 1 minute. Do not over beat.
- Spread into an 8" (20 cm) square pan, lightly sprayed with nonstick cooking spray.

Mexican Roast Chicken with Corn Bread Stuffing

Continued

- Bake corn bread for 20 to 25 minutes. Cool.
- In a heavy frying pan over medium heat, cook bacon for 2 minutes.
- Add the margarine, onions and celery. Cook for 5 minutes. Remove from heat.
- Add 4 cups (1 L) corn bread cut into 1" (2.5 cm) cubes.
- Sprinkle with salt, pepper and poultry seasoning. Stir well.
- Add chicken stock and mix well.
- Preheat oven to 375°F (190°C).
- To prepare chicken, rinse chicken thoroughly. Pat dry with paper towel, inside and out.
- Stuff cavity with corn bread stuffing.
- Place chicken on a rack in a roasting pan.
- Squeeze lime half over chicken; sprinkle with chili powder, cumin, salt and pepper.
- Place the chicken in the oven; roast for 2 hours 15 minutes, or until meat thermometer registers 185°F (85°C).
- To prepare the gravy, remove the chicken from the roaster. Drain off fat. In a bowl, combine cornstarch and vegetable juice. Add to the roaster, stirring constantly. Cook until thickened. Serve on the side.

* It is best to make the corn bread the day before.

Yield: 6 servings

Serving Size: 4 oz. (100 g) chicken, ⅓ cup (75 mL) stuffing

Preparation Time: 25 minutes

Nutritional Analysis

per serving

Calories	500
Protein	31.5 g
Carbohydrate	43.8 g
Fiber	3.5 g
Sugar	6.7 g
Fat	21.5 g
Cholesterol	114.3 mg
Saturated Fat	5.4 g
Mono Fat	6.9 g
Poly Fat	5.3 g
Folate	42 Ug
Vitamin C	12 mg
Sodium	1259 mg
Potassium	485 mg
Iron	3 mg
Calcium	269 mg

Grilled Lemon and Oregano Chicken Breasts

| 6 | boneless, skinless chicken breast halves (3 whole breasts) | 6 |

Lemon and Oil Marinade

¼ cup	olive oil	50 mL
¼ cup	lemon juice	50 mL
1 tbsp.	crushed oregano	15 mL

Lemon, Oregano, Garlic Seasoning

½	lemon	½
1 tbsp.	olive oil	15 mL
1 tbsp.	oregano	15 mL
1	garlic clove, crushed	1
½ tsp.	seasoning salt	2 mL
	freshly ground pepper to taste	

- In a glass dish, marinate chicken in olive oil, lemon juice and crushed oregano for 2 to 6 hours.
- Discard marinade.
- Barbecue over medium-high heat for 6 minutes each side, or until no traces of pink show, OR broil chicken in the oven on a broiler rack, 6" (15 mm) from heat.
- Remove chicken to a warmed serving dish.
- Squeeze lemon half over chicken, sprinkle with olive oil, oregano, garlic, seasoning salt and ground pepper.
- Toss chicken to coat.

Serve with rice and Baby Greens with Fresh Lemon Dressing salad, page 45, or in a warmed pita half with sliced cucumber and tomatoes.

Pictured on page 159.

Yield: 6 servings
Serving Size: 1 half
  chicken breast
Preparation Time:
  10 minutes

Nutritional Analysis
per serving

Calories	207
Protein	26.9 g
Carbohydrate	1.5 g
Fiber	.2 g
Sugar	.2 g
Fat	9.9 g
Cholesterol	73 mg
Saturated Fat	1.8 g
Mono Fat	6.1 g
Poly Fat	1.3 g
Folate	4 Ug
Vitamin C	4 mg
Sodium	190 mg
Potassium	250 mg
Iron	1 mg
Calcium	29 mg

Spinach and Brie Rolled in Chicken Breasts

¼ cup	all-purpose flour	50 mL
½ tsp.	paprika	2 mL
¼ tsp.	lemon pepper	1 mL
dash	nutmeg	
dash	cayenne	
4	chicken breasts, halved, skinned, boned (2 whole breasts)	4
16-20	fresh spinach leaves, stems removed, blanched	16-20
2 oz.	Brie cheese cut into 4 equal pieces	60 g
1 tbsp.	olive oil	15 mL
2	garlic cloves, crushed	2

- Preheat oven to 375°F (190°C).
- In a bowl, mix together flour, paprika, lemon pepper, nutmeg and cayenne. Set aside.
- Pound chicken breasts to ¼" (6 mm) thickness between 2 sheets of waxed paper.
- Lay 4 to 5 spinach leaves on each breast. Place 1 piece of Brie on each.
- Roll up chicken breasts, jelly roll style, tucking in ends if possible to enclose the spinach and Brie. Use toothpicks to secure rolls.
- Roll chickens in flour mixture to coat.
- Heat olive oil over medium heat in a nonstick frying pan. Add garlic and sauté, stirring to release garlic aroma. Remove garlic and add chicken.
- Brown chicken on all sides for 4 minutes total. Remove chicken to a 7 x 11" (17 x 28 cm) baking dish. Bake for 30 minutes.
- Remove toothpicks before serving.

Serve with Lemon Pepper Fettuccine and a steamed vegetable.

Yield: 4 servings
Serving Size: 1 roll
Preparation Time:
  15 minutes

Nutritional Analysis
per serving

Calories	223
Protein	16.7 g
Carbohydrate	8.5 g
Fiber	1.5 g
Sugar	.1 g
Fat	13.8 g
Cholesterol	39.2 mg
Saturated Fat	3.3 g
Mono Fat	6.3 g
Poly Fat	1.5 g
Folate	87 Ug
Vitamin C	6 mg
Sodium	174 mg
Potassium	381 mg
Iron	3 mg
Calcium	100 mg

Chicken in Roasted Red Pepper Sauce

½ cup	all-purpose flour	125 mL
1 tsp.	paprika	5 mL
½ tsp.	thyme	2 mL
dash	cayenne	dash
3 lbs.	chicken pieces	1.5 kg
1 tbsp.	olive oil	15 mL
2	red peppers	2
½ cup	chopped shallots	125 mL
1	garlic clove, chopped	1
1 tsp.	olive oil	5 mL
½ cup	chicken stock, page 43	125 mL
1 tsp.	seasoning salt	5 mL
	hot pepper sauce (optional)	

- In a bag, combine flour, paprika, thyme and cayenne. Add chicken and toss to coat.
- In a large frying pan, over medium heat, brown chicken in 1 tbsp. (15 mL) of oil, about 4 minutes each side.
- Reduce heat to low while making pepper sauce.
- Preheat broiler.
- Wash and dry peppers. Place peppers on a roasting rack 4" (10 cm) from heat.
- Broil 4 minutes each side, or until peppers are blistered and blackened all round. Remove; place in a paper bag to sweat for about 15 minutes.
- In a small frying pan, sauté shallots and garlic in 1 tsp. (5 mL) oil over medium-low heat for 3 minutes.
- Remove red peppers from bag. Cut in half, remove seeds and skin.
- Place peppers into blender or processor. Add shallots and garlic, chicken stock and salt. Purée until smooth. Add hot red pepper sauce to taste, if you wish.
- Pour sauce over chicken. Cover; cook 45 minutes, until chicken is cooked near bone. Stir occasionally.

Serve with steamed zucchini.

Yield: 4 servings
Serving Size:
  2 pieces each
Preparation Time:
  40 minutes

Nutritional Analysis
per serving

Calories	453
Protein	44.3 g
Carbohydrate	15.8 g
Fiber	2 g
Sugar	2.4 g
Fat	22.7 g
Cholesterol	131.7 mg
Saturated Fat	5.6 g
Mono Fat	10.3 g
Poly Fat	4.5 g
Folate	15 Ug
Vitamin C	65 mg
Sodium	463 mg
Potassium	559 mg
Iron	3 mg
Calcium	36 mg

Chicken Paprika

This Hungarian classic has a well-deserved reputation; the chicken is very tender, with a rich, mellow flavor.

2 tbsp.	margarine	25 mL
1	onion, chopped	1
2	garlic cloves, crushed	2
1 tbsp.	Hungarian paprika*	15 mL
½ tsp.	seasoning salt	2 mL
¼ tsp.	black pepper	1 mL
10	chicken pieces (3 lbs. [1.5 kg]), skinned	10
1½ cups	chicken stock, page 43	375 mL
1½ cups	whole small mushrooms	375 mL
1 tbsp.	all-purpose flour	15 mL
½ cup	sour cream	125 mL

- In a large heavy frying pan, over medium heat, melt margarine.
- Add onion, sauté for 3 minutes, until onions are becoming transparent.
- Add garlic, paprika, seasoning salt and pepper. Cook for 2 minutes.
- Add chicken, fry for 4 minutes per side.
- Stir in stock; reduce heat to low; cover and cook for 1 hour, or until chicken is tender, adding mushrooms after ½ hour of cooking.
- In a bowl, mix flour with sour cream. Add to frying pan, stirring well. Heat through but don't boil.

Serve with Cottage Cheese and Noodles with caraway seed garnish, page 127, a salad and caraway rye bread.

* Available in both sweet and hot varieties, Hungarian paprika has a more intense flavor than regular paprika.

Yield: 5 servings
Serving Size: 2 pieces
Preparation Time:
 20 minutes

Nutritional Analysis
per serving

Calories	456
Protein	50.1 g
Carbohydrate	7.4 g
Fiber	1.2 g
Sugar	1.2 g
Fat	24.2 g
Cholesterol	153.1 mg
Saturated Fat	7.6 g
Mono Fat	8.8 g
Poly Fat	5.4 g
Folate	26 Ug
Vitamin C	4 mg
Sodium	576 mg
Potassium	650 mg
Iron	3 mg
Calcium	65 mg

Curried Pineapple Chicken

Curry, mustard and honey add a sweet, spicy tang to this very easy-to-prepare chicken dish. The chicken does not have to be browned before baking.

4	boneless chicken breast halves (2 whole breasts)	4
8 oz.	can crushed pineapple	227 mL
2 tbsp.	honey	25 mL
1 tbsp.	prepared mustard	15 mL
1 tsp.	curry powder	5 mL
½ tsp.	salt	2 mL
½ tsp.	ground ginger	2 mL
⅛ tsp.	black pepper	0.5 mL

- Preheat oven to 350°F (180°C).
- Lightly spray an 8 x 12" (20 x 30 cm) baking dish with nonstick cooking spray.
- Lay chicken breasts in dish.
- In a bowl, combine pineapple, honey, mustard, curry, salt, ginger and pepper. Pour over chicken.
- Cover and bake for 30 minutes.
- Remove the cover and bake the chicken for another 30 minutes, or until the chicken is no longer pink in the center.

Nutrition Tips:

Protein and fat are not good precompetition choices because they take longer to digest and can't be of much use for energy for that activity.

Yield: 4 servings
Serving Size: 1 half chicken breast
Preparation Time: 15 minutes

Nutritional Analysis
per serving

Calories	190
Protein	11.7 g
Carbohydrate	21.1 g
Fiber	.4 g
Sugar	20 g
Fat	6.6 g
Cholesterol	25 mg
Saturated Fat	.3 g
Mono Fat	2.8 g
Poly Fat	1 g
Folate	7 Ug
Vitamin C	7 mg
Sodium	370 mg
Potassium	141 mg
Iron	1 mg
Calcium	13 mg

Baked Chicken Fingers

1 lb.	boned, skinless chicken breasts	500 g
1	egg	1
1 tbsp.	water	15 mL
½ cup	dry bread crumbs	125 mL
¼ cup	cornmeal	50 mL
2 tbsp.	Parmesan cheese	25 mL
1½ tsp.	Cajun seasoning*	7 mL
1 tsp.	paprika	5 mL
¼ cup	whole-wheat flour	50 mL

- Preheat oven to 400°F (200°C).
- Slice chicken into ½" (1 cm) wide strips and set aside.
- In a pie plate, combine egg and water.
- In a shallow dish, prepare coating by combining bread crumbs, cornmeal, cheese, seasoning and paprika.
- In another small bowl, toss chicken fingers in flour to coat; shake off excess flour.
- Dip chicken fingers in egg, then in bread-crumb mixture.
- Arrange chicken on a foil-lined baking sheet that has been sprayed with a nonstick cooking spray.
- Bake 7 minutes, remove tray from oven, turn fingers and return to oven for another 5 minutes.

Serve with honey mustard, plum sauce or barbecue sauce for dipping.

* Any seasoning mix may be substituted. Make your own blend with mixed herbs and ½ tsp. (2 mL) salt.

Yield: 4 servings (24 fingers)
Serving Size: 6 fingers
Preparation Time: 15 minutes

Nutritional Analysis
per serving

Calories	378
Protein	31.2 g
Carbohydrate	23.2 g
Fiber	2 g
Sugar	.7 g
Fat	17.3 g
Cholesterol	111.7 mg
Saturated Fat	1.9 g
Mono Fat	7.1 g
Poly Fat	2.8 g
Folate	23 Ug
Vitamin C	2 mg
Sodium	374 mg
Potassium	346 mg
Iron	2 mg
Calcium	80 mg

Chicken and Stuffing Dinner

2 tbsp.	butter	25 mL
½	medium onion, diced	½
1	celery stalk, diced	1
½ cup	finely chopped mushrooms	125 mL
3 cups	dry ¼" (6 mm) bread cubes	750 mL
½ cup	chicken stock, page 43	125 mL
1 tsp.	poultry seasoning	5 mL
⅛ tsp.	pepper	0.5 mL
4	skinless, boneless chicken breast halves, (2 whole breasts) approximately 1 lb. (500 g)	4
	seasoning salt	
	paprika	

- Preheat oven to 400°F (200°C).
- In a small frying pan, over medium heat, melt butter.
- Add onions, celery and mushrooms. Sauté 3 minutes.
- In a large bowl, mix bread cubes and sautéed vegetables.
- Pour chicken stock over bread cubes. Mix.
- Add poultry seasoning and pepper. Mix well.
- Lightly spray a 7 x 11" (17 x 28 cm) baking dish with nonstick cooking spray.
- Pile stuffing down the middle of the dish lengthwise. Lay chicken breasts to each side of stuffing. Sprinkle chicken lightly with seasoning salt and paprika.
- Cover with foil and bake 20 minutes. Uncover and bake another 15 minutes, or until chicken is no longer pink inside.

Serve with cranberry sauce.

Yield: 4 servings
Serving Size: 1 half chicken breast and ¾ cup (175 mL) dressing
Preparation Time: 15 minutes

Nutritional Analysis
per serving

Calories	271
Protein	29.4 g
Carbohydrate	13.7 g
Fiber	1.2 g
Sugar	1.5 g
Fat	10.2 g
Cholesterol	89.4 mg
Saturated Fat	5 g
Mono Fat	3.2 g
Poly Fat	1.2 g
Folate	19 Ug
Vitamin C	2 mg
Sodium	347 mg
Potassium	361 mg
Iron	2 mg
Calcium	56 mg

Creamy Chicken and Vegetables

An old-fashioned dish with delicious creamy flavor and low-fat ingredients.

3 lb.	chicken cut up (breast cut into 4), skin removed	1.5 kg
½ cup	water	125 mL
1	onion, quartered then cut in half crosswise	1
3	garlic cloves, halved	3
½ tsp.	salt	2 mL
¼ tsp.	black pepper	1 mL
1½ cups	fresh OR frozen whole green beans	375 mL
2	large carrots, cut into diagonal ½" (1 cm)slices	2
10	baby red potatoes, halved	10
¼ cup	chopped fresh dillweed	50 mL
2 tbsp.	all-purpose flour	25 mL
1 cup	2% evaporated milk*	250 mL

- In a large deep frying pan or Dutch oven, combine chicken pieces, water, onion, garlic, salt and pepper.
- Bring to a boil over medium-high heat, reduce to a simmer. Cover and simmer for 30 minutes.
- Add green beans, carrots, potatoes and dillweed. Cover and simmer for 1 hour.
- Mix flour with milk, shake or whisk well.
- Add to chicken and vegetables. Stir well.
- Increase heat to medium. Cook until thickened, stirring occasionally.

Serve with Potato Biscuits, page 23.

* 2% evaporated milk is used for creamy texture without added calories. Substitute whole milk or light (cereal) cream if you prefer.

Yield: 5 servings
Serving Size: 2 pieces
Preparation Time:
 10 minutes;
 cooking time
 1½ hours

Nutritional Analysis

per serving

Calories	352
Protein	37.6 g
Carbohydrate	38.9 g
Fiber	4.2 g
Sugar	5.7 g
Fat	4.8 g
Cholesterol	86.3 mg
Saturated Fat	1.7 g
Mono Fat	1.5 g
Poly Fat	.9 g
Folate	40 Ug
Vitamin C	30 mg
Sodium	380 mg
Potassium	1030 mg
Iron	2 mg
Calcium	200 mg

Paella

This easy version of one of the most popular Spanish dishes is full of color and delicious flavors. In the traditional versions, saffron rice can be combined with chicken, duck, rabbit, cod, mussels, clams, lobster, shrimp, pork, etc. Try other meat and/or shellfish combinations to suit your taste.

3 tbsp.	olive oil	50 mL
½ lb.	boneless chicken breasts	250 g
½ lb.	hot OR mild Italian sausage, in ½" (1 cm) slices	250 g
1	medium onion, chopped	1
1	green OR red pepper, chopped	1
2	celery stalks, chopped	2
2	garlic cloves, minced	2
½ tsp.	crushed basil	2 mL
½ tsp.	crushed oregano	2 mL
½ tsp.	turmeric	2 mL
½ tsp.	paprika	2 mL
pinch	cayenne pepper (more if you like it hot)	pinch
1 cup	long-grain rice	250 mL
14 oz.	can diced tomatoes with herbs	398 mL
1 cup	chicken stock, page 43	250 mL
½ cup	frozen green peas	125 mL
½ lb.	large shrimp, shelled, deveined	250 g
12	whole spiced black olives* (not California-style)	12
	Cajun seasoning OR salt and pepper to taste	
1	green onion, sliced	1

- In a large heavy frying pan, heat oil over medium heat.
- Add chicken and Italian sausage. Brown on all sides for 10 minutes.
- Remove the chicken and sausage from the heat to a side plate.

Paella

Continued

- To the frying pan, add onion, pepper and celery. Sauté for 5 minutes, or until vegetables are browned.
- Add garlic, basil, oregano, turmeric, paprika and cayenne. Sauté for 2 minutes.
- Stir in the rice and sauté for 3 minutes.
- Add the tomatoes and chicken stock. Bring to a boil; reduce heat to a simmer.
- Cut the sausage into ½" (1 cm) slices and the chicken into 1" (2.5 cm) pieces. Add to the rice mixture. Cover and cook for 20 minutes, or until most of the liquid is absorbed.
- Add peas, shrimp and olives, Cover and cook for another 10 minutes, or until the shrimp are opaque.
- Remove the paella from the heat. Let stand for 10 minutes.
- Season with Cajun seasoning or salt and pepper. Sprinkle with sliced green onions.

Serve with Tomato and Mushroom Salad, page 53.

* Use Spanish, Italian or Greek spiced black olives – the tinned California black olives have a very different flavor.

Yield: 6 servings

Serving Size: 1½ cups (375 mL)

Preparation Time: 1 hour

Nutritional Analysis

per serving

Calories	382
Protein	27.2 g
Carbohydrate	17.2 g
Fiber	1.9 g
Sugar	4.7 g
Fat	21.8 g
Cholesterol	64.1 mg
Saturated Fat	5.1 g
Mono Fat	10.2 g
Poly Fat	2.3 g
Folate	18 Ug
Vitamin C	17 mg
Sodium	856 mg
Potassium	295 mg
Iron	2 mg
Calcium	90 mg

Nutrition Tips:

Did you know that fluid losses due to sweating can exceed 4 pounds (2 L) an hour.

Mixed Bean and Chicken Chili

1 tbsp.	olive oil	15 mL
2	skinless, boneless chicken breast halves, diced	2
1	medium onion, chopped	1
½	green pepper, diced	½
2	celery stalks, sliced	2
2	garlic cloves, crushed	2
2 tbsp.	chili powder	25 mL
19 oz.	can diced tomatoes	540 mL
2.5 oz.	can peeled, chopped green chilies	127 mL
1 cup	chicken stock, page 43	250 mL
19 oz.	can mixed beans, drained	540 mL
2 tsp.	granulated sugar	10 mL

- In a large saucepan, heat oil over medium-high heat.
- Add chicken; cook until lightly browned.
- Add onion, green pepper, celery and garlic. Cook for 4 minutes, stirring occasionally.
- Add chili powder; cook and stir for 1 minute.
- Add tomatoes, green chilies and chicken stock.
- Reduce the heat to low; cover and simmer for 15 minutes.
- Add beans and sugar. Simmer for 15 minutes, uncovered.

Serve over rice and with Cool Cucumber Salad, page 49.

Chicken

Grilled Lemon and Oregano Chicken Breast, page 148

Tomato and Mushroom Salad, page 53

Yield: 4 servings
Serving Size: 1 cup (250 mL)
Preparation Time: 20 minutes

Nutritional Analysis
per serving

Calories	167
Protein	12.8 g
Carbohydrate	19.9 g
Fiber	6.5 g
Sugar	4.4 g
Fat	4.7 g
Cholesterol	22.1 mg
Saturated Fat	1 g
Mono Fat	1.8 g
Poly Fat	.8 g
Folate	67 Ug
Vitamin C	22 mg
Sodium	402 mg
Potassium	558 mg
Iron	2 mg
Calcium	79 mg

Tarragon Chicken and Rice

2 tbsp.	margarine	25 mL
½ cup	diced onion	125 mL
⅓ cup	sliced celery	75 mL
1	garlic clove, minced	1
1½ cups	mushroom soup**, page 41	375 mL
½ tsp.	crushed tarragon	2 mL
¼ tsp.	poultry seasoning	1 mL
	freshly ground pepper to taste	
2 cups	cooked brown rice*	500 mL
1 cup	diced, cooked chicken	250 mL
½ cup	grated Cheddar cheese	125 mL

- Preheat oven to 350°F (180°C).
- In a medium saucepan, over medium heat, melt margarine. Add onion, celery and garlic. Sauté for 5 minutes.
- Add soup, tarragon, poultry seasoning and pepper. Mix well.
- Cook, stirring occasionally, until mixture is hot and thickened.
- Lightly spray a 6-cup (1.5 L) casserole with non-stick cooking spray.
- Mix rice and chicken together in the casserole.
- Stir in the soup mixture.
- Sprinkle the casserole with grated Cheddar cheese.
- Bake for 20 minutes, until bubbling.
- Let stand for 5 to 10 minutes before serving.

* Brown rice takes 15 to 30 minutes more to cook than does white rice. The 1 to 2, water to rice proportions are the same.

** If using canned mushroom soup, add ½ cup (125 mL) 1% milk or water.

Variations: One 6.5 oz. (184 g) can of flaked chicken may be substituted for diced chicken.

Yield: 5 servings
Serving Size: 1 cup
 (250 mL)
Preparation Time:
 15 minutes

Nutritional Analysis
per serving

Calories	283
Protein	15.7 g
Carbohydrate	25.3 g
Fiber	2.3 g
Sugar	3.2 g
Fat	13.2 g
Cholesterol	43.7 mg
Saturated Fat	5.5 g
Mono Fat	4.4 g
Poly Fat	2.6 g
Folate	19 Ug
Vitamin C	3 mg
Sodium	326 mg
Potassium	300 mg
Iron	1 mg
Calcium	154 mg

Turkey Sausage and Vegetable Stew with Cheese Roll Topping

2 cups	1" (2.5 cm) cubes of squash (butternut, buttercup, acorn, etc.)	500 mL
1½ cups	1" (2.5 cm) cubes of turnips	375 mL
2	large carrots, ¼" (6 mm) slices	2
2	parsnips, peeled, ¼" (6 mm) slices	2
2	celery stalks, ¼" (6 mm) slices	2
4	small red potatoes, scrubbed, quartered lengthwise then halved crosswise	4
1	medium onion, chopped	1
6	garlic cloves, minced	6
2 tbsp.	canola oil	25 mL
28 oz.	can diced tomatoes	796 mL
½ cup	water	125 mL
¾ lb.	smoked turkey sausage, ¼" (6 mm) slices	350 g
1 tsp.	poultry seasoning	5 mL
1 tsp.	salt	5 mL
½ tsp.	black pepper	2 mL
2 tbsp.	all-purpose flour	25 mL

Cheese Roll Topping

2 cups	all-purpose flour	500 mL
4 tsp.	baking powder	20 mL
½ tsp.	salt	2 mL
⅓ cup	cold margarine	75 mL
⅔ cup	2% milk	150 mL
1 cup	grated Cheddar cheese	250 mL

- Prepare vegetables.
- Heat oil in a large Dutch oven over medium heat.
- Add squash, turnip, carrots, parsnips, celery, potatoes, onion and garlic. Cook, stirring occasionally, for 15 minutes. Reduce heat so they brown do but not scorch.

Turkey Sausage and Vegetable Stew with Cheese Roll Topping

Continued

- Add diced tomatoes, water, sausage, poultry seasoning, salt and pepper.
- Cover; reduce heat to a gentle simmer and cook 1½ hours, stirring occasionally, until all vegetables are tender.
- In a small pan, over medium heat, brown flour, stirring constantly for 2 minutes.
- While stirring stew, sprinkle in browned flour, increase heat to medium and cook just until liquid thickens, stirring well. Turn off heat, cover while making cheese roll topping.
- Stew can be made to this point, cooled and refrigerated for 1 to 2 days.
- When ready to use, reheat on the stove in a Dutch oven, then transfer to a 10-cup (2.5 L) casserole.
- To prepare the cheese rolls, preheat oven to 425°F (220°C).
- Mix flour, baking powder and salt in a bowl.
- Cut in margarine until crumbly.
- With a fork, stir in milk until flour is mixed in. Lightly knead 4 to 5 times on a floured surface.
- Roll out to 8 x 12" (20 x 30 cm), ¼" (6 mm) thick.
- Sprinkle cheese on top.
- Roll up jelly roll style from the long side. Cut into 1" (2.5 cm) slices.
- Place cheese roll slices on top of hot stew in casserole, leaving a space between each roll.
- Bake for 20 to 25 minutes, until cheese rolls are browned on top.
- To serve, use a big scoop to spoon out stew, top each serving with 1 to 2 cheese rolls.

Yield:
6 servings
Serving Size:
1½ cups (375 mL)
Preparation Time:
40 minutes

Nutritional Analysis
per serving

Calories	476
Protein	18.6 g
Carbohydrate	58 g
Fiber	6.8 g
Sugar	11.5 g
Fat	20.4 g
Cholesterol	43 mg
Saturated Fat	5.7 g
Mono Fat	5.9 g
Poly Fat	5.1 g
Folate	58 Ug
Vitamin C	31 mg
Sodium	1495 mg
Potassium	689 mg
Iron	4 mg
Calcium	388 mg

Thai Turkey Meatballs

1 lb.	lean ground turkey breast	500 g
8 oz.	can sliced water chestnuts, finely chopped	227 mL
1 cup	fresh bread crumbs	250 mL
1	egg	1
2	green onions, finely chopped	2
1½ tsp.	sesame seed oil, divided	7 mL
2 tsp.	canola oil, divided	10 mL
6 tbsp.	liquid honey OR creamed honey, melted	90 mL
¼ cup	soy sauce	50 mL
2 tsp.	crushed fresh ginger	10 mL
2 tsp.	cornstarch	10 mL
¼ cup	water	50 mL
10	garlic cloves, crushed	10
1 tsp.	crushed red chili flakes	5 mL
1	red bell pepper, cut into ½" (1 cm) squares	1
	basmati OR jasmine rice for 6	

- In a bowl, combine ground turkey breast, chopped water chestnuts, bread crumbs, egg, green onion, ½ tsp. (2 mL) sesame oil. Stir well.
- Using an ⅛ cup (25 mL) measure, scoop up meat mixture, making into meatballs.
- Heat 1 tsp. (5 mL) of oil in a nonstick frying pan; add meatballs and cook until browned on all sides, about 5 minutes. Reduce heat to medium-low; cover and cook for 10 minutes.
- In a small bowl, mix honey, soy sauce, ginger, cornstarch and water. Set aside.
- Remove meatballs from frying pan.
- Heat 1 tsp. (5 mL) EACH sesame oil and canola oil. Add garlic and chilies. Stir. Add red pepper; cook and stir for 5 minutes. Do not brown.
- Add cornstarch mixture and meatballs. Cook and stir until hot, sauce is thickened and clear.

Serve over steamed rice.

Yield: 6 servings
Serving Size: 3 meatballs Preparation Time:
25 minutes

Nutritional Analysis
per serving

Calories	326
Protein	17 g
Carbohydrate	40.3 g
Fiber	2.9 g
Sugar	20 g
Fat	11.7 g
Cholesterol	99.6 mg
Saturated Fat	2.9 g
Mono Fat	4.3 g
Poly Fat	3.1 g
Folate	21 Ug
Vitamin C	16 mg
Sodium	924 mg
Potassium	276 mg
Iron	4 mg
Calcium	171 mg

Marinated Broiled Lamb Chops

1	lemon, thinly sliced	1
½	medium onion, finely chopped	½
2 tsp.	crushed dried mint	10 mL
2	garlic cloves, crushed	2
1 tsp.	seasoning salt	5 mL
1 tsp.	paprika	5 mL
½ tsp.	black pepper	2 mL
8	lamb chops	8

- In a large heavy freezer bag, combine lemon, onion, mint, garlic, seasoning salt, paprika and pepper.
- Add lamb chops, massage marinade into chops well with hands, squeezing through the outside of the bag. Be careful not to puncture the bag with the chop bones.
- Refrigerate chops for 12 hours up to 2 days, massaging periodically.
- Remove chops 30 minutes before cooking. Remove from marinade. Place on a broiling rack.
- Preheat broiler.
- Broil chops 4" (10 cm) from heat for 5 to 6 minutes per side. Chops should still be slightly pink inside.

Serve with Tabbouleh, page 47, or Baby Greens with Fresh Lemon Dressing, page 45.

Yield: 4 servings
Serving Size: 2 chops
Preparation Time:
  10 minutes

Nutritional Analysis
per serving

Calories	477
Protein	28.9 g
Carbohydrate	3.7 g
Fiber	.9 g
Sugar	.7 g
Fat	38.1 g
Cholesterol	126.8 mg
Saturated Fat	16.3 g
Mono Fat	15.5 g
Poly Fat	3.1 g
Folate	23 Ug
Vitamin C	11 mg
Sodium	440 mg
Potassium	415 mg
Iron	3 mg
Calcium	39 mg

Roast Pork with Creamy Herbed Gravy

3 lb.	rib end pork loin roast, boned, rolled	1.5 kg
½ tsp.	EACH crushed rosemary, thyme dry mustard, freshly ground pepper, paprika	2 mL
1	large garlic clove	1

Creamy Herbed Gravy

4 tsp.	all-purpose flour	20 mL
¼ tsp.	EACH crushed rosemary, crushed thyme, black pepper, salt	1 mL
1½ cups	1% milk	375 mL
2 tsp.	Dijon mustard	10 mL

- Preheat oven to 350°F (180°C).
- Place the roast on a rack in a roasting pan.
- In a small bowl, combine rosemary, thyme, dry mustard, pepper and paprika.
- Slice garlic into 4 with the tip of a sharp knife.
- Poke 4 holes into the meat, 1½" (4 cm) deep. Push a slice of garlic into each.
- With fingers, sprinkle and rub the seasoning all over the roast. Insert meat thermometer.
- Roast, uncovered, for 1 hour. Cover and roast another hour. Remove lid and roast for 15 minutes, until internal temperature reads 170°F (80°C). Let rest for 15 minutes before carving.
- To make gravy, in a jar with a tight fitting lid, shake flour, rosemary, thyme, pepper, salt and milk until well blended.
- Remove roast to carving tray. Pour milk mixture into roasting pan, heat over medium heat, stirring to loosen drippings.
- Reduce heat to low once gravy has thickened. Stir in Dijon mustard.
- Cover and keep warm until serving. When ready to serve, pour gravy into a heated gravy boat.

Yield: 8 servings
Serving Size: 2 slices of pork, ¼ cup (50 mL) gravy
Preparation Time: 20 minutes

Nutritional Analysis
per serving

Calories	449
Protein	32.7 g
Carbohydrate	3.8 g
Fiber	.2 g
Sugar	2.1 g
Fat	32.7 g
Cholesterol	78.2 mg
Saturated Fat	11.9 g
Mono Fat	14.9 g
Poly Fat	3.7 g
Folate	12 Ug
Vitamin C	1 mg
Sodium	159 mg
Potassium	543 mg
Iron	2 mg
Calcium	77 mg

Curried Peanut Butter Pork Chops

2 tsp.	canola oil	10 mL
4, ¾"	thick pork loin chops	4, 1.8 cm
1 tsp.	salt	5 mL
½ tsp.	curry powder	2 mL
1	small onion, sliced	1
½	red pepper, cut in strips	½
1	small zucchini, diced	1
4 cups	cooked long-grain rice and wild rice	1 L
2 tbsp.	peanut butter, crunchy OR smooth	25 mL
¼ cup	warm water	50 mL

- In a large nonstick frying pan, heat oil over medium heat.
- Add pork chops, brown for 5 minutes on 1 side and 3 to 4 minutes on the other side.
- Remove pork chops to a dish and keep warm.
- Reduce heat to medium low. Add salt and curry powder to frying pan. Stir and heat.
- Add onion and red pepper.
- Cook and stir 1 minute.
- Return pork chops to frying pan, along with any juices in the dish.
- Cover and cook for 35 minutes, adding zucchini halfway through.
- Meanwhile, cook the rice as per package directions.
- Spoon cooked rice onto a serving platter; lay pork chops and vegetables on top. Keep warm.
- Blend peanut butter and warm water. Stir into frying pan. Heat to boiling. Pour peanut sauce over chops.

Variation: Add a few drops of hot red pepper sauce or red pepper flakes to the peanut sauce if you wish.

Yield: 4 servings
Serving Size: 1 chop
  plus 1¼ cups (300 mL)
  of rice mixture
Preparation Time:
  50 minutes

Nutritional Analysis
per serving

Calories	183
Protein	17.3 g
Carbohydrate	5.1 g
Fiber	1.5 g
Sugar	2 g
Fat	10.7 g
Cholesterol	36.1 mg
Saturated Fat	2.4 g
Mono Fat	3.8 g
Poly Fat	2.3 g
Folate	23 Ug
Vitamin C	13 mg
Sodium	662 mg
Potassium	485 mg
Iron	1 mg
Calcium	29 mg

Pork Chow Mein

1½ cups	chicken OR beef stock, page 44	375 mL
4 cups	dry chow mein noodles*	1 L
2 cups	fresh bean sprouts	500 mL
1 tbsp.	canola oil	15 mL
¾ lb.	pork steak, in ½" (1 cm) cubes	350 g
1 cup	sliced celery, diagonally cut in ¼" (6 mm) slices	250 mL
½ cup	sliced fresh mushrooms	125 mL
2 tbsp.	soy sauce	25 mL
1 tbsp.	granulated sugar	15 mL
4	green onions, diagonally cut into ¼" (6 mm) slices	4
1 tbsp.	cornstarch	15 mL
¼ cup	cold water	50 mL
¼ cup	chopped, roasted cashews	50 mL

- In wok or large deep frying pan, heat 1 cup (250 mL) stock over medium-low heat. Add noodles and bean sprouts. Cook, covered, for 2 to 3 minutes.
- Place softened noodles on a serving platter. Keep warm in oven.
- Add oil to work. Heat over medium-high heat. Brown pork cubes, stirring constantly. Add celery and mushrooms. Cook and stir 2 minutes.
- To remaining stock, add soy sauce and sugar. Add to wok, reduce heat and simmer, covered, for 10 minutes.
- Add onions, simmer another 5 minutes.
- Blend cornstarch with water. Stir into wok. Cook until sauce is clear and slightly thickened.

Serve over hot noodles. Sprinkle with cashews.

* Western chow mein noodles are crispy deep-fried noodles

Yield: 6 servings
Serving Size: 1⅓ cups (325 mL)
Preparation Time: 35 minutes

Nutritional Analysis
per serving

Calories	344
Protein	21 g
Carbohydrate	31.1 g
Fiber	3.5 g
Sugar	3.3 g
Fat	15.3 g
Cholesterol	31.9 mg
Saturated Fat	3.2 g
Mono Fat	11.2 g
Poly Fat	1.2 g
Folate	44 Ug
Vitamin C	9 mg
Sodium	685 mg
Potassium	369 mg
Iron	3 mg
Calcium	39 mg

Ham and Bean Bake

Easy, easy, easy – a family-tested, one-dish meal using on-hand ingredients.

1 lb.	ham steak, cut into ½" (1 cm) cubes	500 g
19 oz.	can white kidney beans, drained	540 mL
14 oz.	can beans in molasses	398 mL
10 oz.	can mushroom stems and pieces	284 mL
8 oz.	can pineapple tidbits	227 mL
5½ oz.	can tomato paste with garlic	156 mL
¾ cup	water	175 mL
¼ cup	brown sugar	50 mL
¼ cup	barbecue sauce	50 mL
1	medium onion, chopped	1
1	celery stalk, chopped	1
½	red pepper, diced	½

- Preheat oven to 350°F (180°C).
- In a large bean pot or Dutch oven, combine ham cubes, kidney beans, beans in molasses, mushrooms, pineapple tidbits, tomato paste, water, brown sugar, barbecue sauce, onions, celery and red pepper.
- Cover and bake for 1½ hours.
- Remove lid and bake for 15 minutes more.

Yield: 8 servings
Serving Size: 1 cup
  (250 mL)
Preparation Time:
  20 minutes

Nutritional Analysis
per serving

Calories	256
Protein	19.3 g
Carbohydrate	38.6 g
Fiber	8.6 g
Sugar	19.4 g
Fat	3.9 g
Cholesterol	28.8 mg
Saturated Fat	1.2 g
Mono Fat	1.5 g
Poly Fat	.6 g
Folate	62 Ug
Vitamin C	14 mg
Sodium	1490 mg
Potassium	624 mg
Iron	3 mg
Calcium	79 mg

Oven Barbecued Ribs with Foil-Wrapped Vegetables

3 lbs.	pork side ribs, breast bone removed	1.5 kg
	freshly ground pepper to taste	
4	small red potatoes, scrubbed, cut into ¼" (6 mm) slices	4
4	carrots, peeled, each cut into 6 diagonal pieces	6
2	green onions, cut into 2" (5 cm) lengths	2
1 tbsp.	olive oil	15 mL
½ tsp.	seasoning salt	2 mL
¼ tsp.	black pepper	1 mL

Red Wine Tomato Sauce

1¼ cups	crushed tomatoes	300 mL
¾ cup	water	175 mL
½ cup	brown sugar	125 mL
¼ cup	red wine vinegar	50 mL
½ tsp.	paprika	2 mL
½ tsp.	chili powder	2 mL
½ tsp.	salt	2 mL
1	garlic clove, crushed	1
¼ tsp.	celery seed	1 mL

- Preheat oven to 350°F (180°C).
- Cut ribs into 4 equal pieces, trimming off any excess fat.
- Lay the ribs in a roasting pan, lightly sprinkle with pepper.
- Bake 45 minutes, turning once.

Oven Barbecued Ribs with Foil-Wrapped Vegetables

Continued

- Prepare vegetable packets while ribs are baking.
- Lay a strip of heavy-duty foil, 1½' (45 cm) long, on the counter.
- Pile the potato slices, carrots and green onions in the center of the foil.
- Drizzle with olive oil. Season with salt and pepper.
- Cover with another 1½' (45 cm) strip of foil, folding the edges together all around to form an 8 x 12" (19 x 30 cm) sealed packet.
- After the ribs have baked for 45 minutes, drain off the fat and cover the roaster.
- Place vegetable packet in the oven.
- Bake ribs for another hour.
- Make the Red Wine Tomato Sauce by combining in a medium saucepan, the crushed tomatoes, water, brown sugar, vinegar, paprika, chili powder, salt, garlic and celery seed.
- Stir and heat over medium heat just until the sauce starts to steam. Remove from the heat.
- Pour the sauce over the ribs; bake, uncovered, for 30 minutes, spooning the sauce over once.
- To serve the vegetables, cut an "X" in the top of the foil packet, pull back the foil and serve the vegetables with the ribs.

Yield: 4 servings
Serving Size: ¼ of the ribs and vegetables
Preparation Time:
25 minutes;
ribs bake 2 hours
15 minutes;
vegetables 1 hour
30 minutes

Nutritional Analysis
per serving

Calories	997
Protein	84.5 g
Carbohydrate	65.5 g
Fiber	6.2 g
Sugar	35 g
Fat	42.7 g
Cholesterol	177.6 mg
Saturated Fat	14 g
Mono Fat	20.1 g
Poly Fat	5.1 g
Folate	38 Ug
Vitamin C	29 mg
Sodium	923 mg
Potassium	1865 mg
Iron	6 mg
Calcium	231 mg

Stuffed Baked Peppers

⅓ cup	tomato paste	75 mL
¾ cup	water	175 mL
1 tsp.	granulated sugar	5 mL
2	large green bell peppers	2
1	small onion, chopped	1
1 tbsp.	canola oil	15 mL
1½ cups	finely chopped cabbage	375 mL
½ lb.	lean ground pork	250 g
1	egg, lightly beaten	1
¼ cup	water	50 mL
⅓ cup	uncooked long-grain rice	75 mL
½ tsp.	salt	2 mL
¼ tsp.	pepper	1 mL

- In a 7 x 11" (17 x 28 cm) baking dish, mix together tomato paste, water and sugar.
- Cut green peppers in half lengthwise, remove ribs and seeds. Place in baking dish and set aside.
- In a frying pan, over medium heat, sauté onion in oil until it starts to turn brown. Add cabbage; cook for 2 minutes and remove from heat.
- In a large bowl, mix together ground pork, egg, water, rice, salt, pepper and cabbage mixture. Mix well.
- Divide mixture among prepared green peppers. Drizzle a spoonful of sauce over each pepper.
- Cover with foil. Bake at 350°F (180°C) for 50 to 60 minutes.
- Spoon tomato sauce over stuffed peppers to serve.

Serve with fresh Italian bread.

Note: Leftover tomato paste can be frozen in 1 tbsp. (15 mL) amounts. Place on waxed paper to freeze then store in a plastic bag. Use these cubes in other recipes.

Yield: 4 servings
Serving Size: ½ pepper
Preparation Time:
20 minutes

Nutritional Analysis
per serving

Calories	233
Protein	9.2 g
Carbohydrate	23.4 g
Fiber	2.5 g
Sugar	6 g
Fat	11.7 g
Cholesterol	70.8 mg
Saturated Fat	3 g
Mono Fat	3.5 g
Poly Fat	2.1 g
Folate	31 Ug
Vitamin C	47 mg
Sodium	607 mg
Potassium	377 mg
Iron	2 mg
Calcium	39 mg

Meat Loaf with Brown Sugar, Mustard Glaze

Serve hot for one meal. Any leftover slices can be served cold on a bun or in a pita for a take-along lunch the next day.

1½ cups	fresh whole-wheat bread crumbs	375 mL
1 cup	1% milk	250 mL
1 lb.	lean ground beef	500 g
1 lb.	lean ground pork	500 g
2	eggs	2
¼ cup	wheat germ	50 mL
½ cup	grated onion	125 mL
¼ cup	ketchup	50 mL
1 tbsp.	Worcestershire sauce	15 mL
1½ tsp.	seasoning salt	7 mL
1	garlic clove, minced	1
½ tsp.	black pepper	2 mL

Brown Sugar Mustard Glaze

¼ cup	brown sugar	50 mL
¼ cup	ketchup	50 mL
1 tsp.	dry mustard	5 mL

- In a large bowl, soak the bread crumbs in milk for 20 minutes.
- Preheat oven to 350°F (180°C).
- To bread crumbs, add beef, pork, eggs, wheat germ, onion, ketchup, Worcestershire sauce, seasoning salt, garlic and pepper. Blend well.
- Turn into a 4½ x 8½" (12 x 21cm) loaf pan lightly sprayed with a nonstick cooking spray.
- To prepare the glaze, combine brown sugar, ketchup and mustard. Spread over meat loaf.
- Bake 1½ to 2 hours, until no pink juices rise when loaf is pierced in the middle with a knife.
- Allow the loaf to sit for 10 minutes.
- Cut into 1" (2.5 cm) slices.

Yield: 8 servings
Serving size: 1"
   (2.5 cm) slice
Preparation Time:
   30 minutes.

Nutritional Analysis
per serving

Calories	372
Protein	21.5 g
Carbohydrate	20.4 g
Fiber	1.2 g
Sugar	11.5 g
Fat	22.5 g
Cholesterol	119.8 mg
Saturated Fat	8 g
Mono Fat	9.6 g
Poly Fat	2.5 g
Folate	29 Ug
Vitamin C	8 mg
Sodium	1170 mg
Potassium	500 mg
Iron	3 mg
Calcium	89 mg

Layered Italian Meat Loaf

1 lb.	lean ground beef	500 g
½ lb.	hot OR mild Italian sausage, removed from casing	250 g
10 oz.	frozen chopped spinach, thawed, squeezed to drain	300 g
2 ½ cups	Basic Tomato Sauce, page 128, divided	625 mL
1	egg	1
½ cup	dry bread crumbs	125 mL
1 tsp.	crushed oregano	5 mL
1	garlic clove, minced	1
4	slices Capicolla* OR Black Forest ham	4
1 cup	grated partly skimmed mozzarella cheese	250 mL
1 tbsp.	brown sugar	15 mL
¼ tsp.	crushed red chili pepper	1 mL

- Preheat oven to 350°C (180°C).
- In a bowl combine ground beef, sausage meat, spinach, ⅓ cup (75 mL) tomato sauce, egg, bread crumbs, oregano and garlic. Mix well.
- Layer half the mixture into a 5 x 7 (12 x 17 cm) loaf pan. Add a layer of the ham slices then cheese. Top with remaining meat mixture. Pat down and smooth top.
- Bake for 1 hour 20 minutes, until juice runs clear when pierced with a knife.
- Prepare a glaze by mixing ⅓ cup (75 mL) tomato sauce, brown sugar and crushed red chili pepper in a small bowl.
- Spoon over meat loaf. Bake for 10 minutes.
- Remove loaf from oven, let rest 10 minutes before serving.
- Cut into 6 thick slices.

Serve with pasta and remaining heated tomato sauce.

* Capicolla or Coppa is a dry, air-cured pork salami. It is very tender, with a delicious mellow taste, more intense than proscuitto.

Yield: 6 servings
Serving Size: 1 slice
Preparation Time: 16 minutes

Nutritional Analysis
per serving

Calories	459
Protein	31 g
Carbohydrate	22.5 g
Fiber	2.8 g
Sugar	8 g
Fat	28.1 g
Cholesterol	130.4 mg
Saturated Fat	10.4 g
Mono Fat	11.2 g
Poly Fat	2.2 g
Folate	97 Ug
Vitamin C	28 mg
Sodium	1354 mg
Potassium	698 mg
Iron	4 mg
Calcium	235 mg

Shepherd's Pie

5	medium potatoes, peeled, quartered	5
¼ cup	milk	50 mL
1 tbsp.	butter	15 mL
1½ lbs.	lean ground beef	750 g
1	medium onion, diced	1
2	garlic cloves, crushed	2
1 tbsp.	all-purpose flour	15 mL
1½ cups	beef stock*, page 44	375 mL
2 cups	chopped fresh OR frozen mixed vegetables	500 mL
10 oz.	can mushroom stems and pieces, drained	284 mL
	pepper to taste	
½ cup	grated Cheddar cheese	125 mL
	paprika	

- Simmer potatoes in boiling salted water until cooked, about 15 minutes. Drain.
- Mash potatoes, adding milk and butter.
- Preheat oven to 350°F (180°C).
- Over medium heat, in a large nonstick frying pan, brown beef, onion and garlic. Drain drippings.
- Add flour, stock, vegetables, mushrooms and pepper. Reduce heat, simmer 5 minutes.
- Turn into a 12-cup (3 L) casserole.
- Top beef mixture with mashed potatoes, spread evenly to cover. Sprinkle with grated cheese and paprika. Bake 30 minutes.

* If you do not have beef stock on hand, use 1½ cups (375 mL) of boiling water and a 1 oz. (25 g) package of brown gravy mix, or leftover beef gravy.

Yield: 6 servings
Serving Size: 1 cup (250 mL)
Preparation Time: 45 minutes

Nutritional Analysis
per serving

Calories	537
Protein	38.5 g
Carbohydrate	38.4 g
Fiber	5.6 g
Sugar	6.5 g
Fat	25.7 g
Cholesterol	124 mg
Saturated Fat	11.3 g
Mono Fat	10.3 g
Poly Fat	1.1 g
Folate	44 Ug
Vitamin C	19 mg
Sodium	517 mg
Potassium	1006 mg
Iron	4 mg
Calcium	124 mg

Chunky Chili Stew

6	slices bacon, diced	6
1 cup	diced onion	250 mL
½	green pepper, diced	½
1	garlic clove, crushed	1
1 lb.	lean ground beef	500 g
1 tbsp.	chili powder	15 mL
1 tsp.	seasoning salt	5 mL
¼ tsp.	crushed chili flakes	1 mL
19 oz.	can diced tomatoes	540 mL
½ cup	water	125 mL
1	celery stalk, chopped	1
2	large carrots, chopped	2
2	medium potatoes, cut into ½" (1 cm) cubes	2
12 oz.	can whole kernel corn	341 mL
14 oz.	can kidney beans, drained	398 mL
14 oz.	beans in molasses	398 mL

- In a large saucepan or Dutch oven, over medium to medium-low heat, sauté bacon until crisp.
- Remove bacon, sauté onion, green pepper and garlic in bacon drippings, until soft.
- Add ground beef, cook until browned, stirring to break up. Drain off excess fat.
- Add chili powder, seasoning salt, crushed chilies, tomatoes and water.
- Add celery, carrots and potato; stir; cover and simmer for 30 minutes.
- Add corn, kidney beans and beans in molasses; stir. Cover and simmer for 30 minutes. Stir in diced bacon.

Serve with Potato Biscuits, page 23. Leftovers can be frozen.

Beef

Chunky Chili Stew, page 176
Potato Biscuits, page 23

Yield: 8 servings
Serving Size: 1¼ cups (300 mL)
Preparation Time: 35 minutes

Nutritional Analysis
per serving

Calories	342
Protein	18.9 g
Carbohydrate	39.3 g
Fiber	9.4 g
Sugar	13.3 g
Fat	12.2 g
Cholesterol	42.5 mg
Saturated Fat	4.5 g
Mono Fat	5.3 g
Poly Fat	1 g
Folate	60 Ug
Vitamin C	21 mg
Sodium	962 mg
Potassium	669 mg
Iron	3 mg
Calcium	91 mg

Beef and Barley Stew

2 lbs.	blade steak, cut into 1" (2.5 cm) cubes	1 kg
2 tbsp.	all-purpose flour	25 mL
2 tbsp.	canola oil	25 mL
1 tsp.	paprika	5 mL
½ tsp.	salt	2 mL
¼ tsp.	ground black pepper	1 mL
1	medium onion, quartered lengthwise, halved crosswise	1
2	garlic cloves, minced	2
2 cups	beef stock*, page 44	500 mL
½ cup	dry red wine OR extra beef stock	125 mL
2 tbsp.	tomato paste	25 mL
⅓ cup	pot barley	75 mL
4	carrots, cut into ¼" (6 mm) slices	4
1½ cups	fresh mushrooms, halved	375 mL
1 tsp.	thyme OR 1½ tsp. (7 mL) rosemary	5 mL

- Preheat oven to 325°F (160°C).
- Toss beef cubes in flour.
- In a large ovenproof pot or Dutch oven, heat oil over medium heat. Cook meat for 7 minutes, stirring occasionally until all red is gone.
- Add paprika, salt and pepper. Stir.
- Add onion and garlic. Cook 2 minutes, stirring occasionally.
- Add beef stock, red wine, tomato paste, barley, carrots, mushrooms and thyme or rosemary. Stir, scraping bottom of pot to loosen bits. Cover.
- Bake for 2 hours, or until the beef is tender.

* Canned beef broth or low-salt beef bouillon dissolved in water may be substituted for beef stock.

Yield: 8 servings
Serving Size: 1 cup (250 mL)
Preparation Time: 30 minutes

Nutritional Analysis
per serving

Calories	263
Protein	20.5 g
Carbohydrate	18.7 g
Fiber	3.3 g
Sugar	4.7 g
Fat	10.9 g
Cholesterol	38.9 mg
Saturated Fat	2.8 g
Mono Fat	3.1 g
Poly Fat	1.6 g
Folate	24 Ug
Vitamin C	8 mg
Sodium	418 mg
Potassium	616 mg
Iron	4 mg
Calcium	35 mg

Mandarin Beef Stir-Fry

¾ lb.	sirloin steak, thinly sliced	350 g
1 tbsp.	Worcestershire sauce	15 mL
4 tsp.	soy sauce	20 mL
1 tsp.	sesame oil	5 mL
1½ tsp.	curry powder	7 mL
¼ tsp.	crushed chilies	1 mL
1	garlic clove, crushed	1
1"	piece of fresh ginger, minced	2.5 cm
	orange juice to make 1 cup (250 mL) with reserved liquid from orange segments	
1 tbsp.	cornstarch	15 mL
1 tbsp.	canola oil	15 mL
4 cups	cauliflower florets	1 L
1	red pepper, in ½" (1 cm) squares	1
3	green onions, in 2" (5 cm) lengths	3
10 oz.	can mandarin orange segments, drained, reserve liquid	284 mL

- In a glass bowl, combine beef, Worcestershire sauce, 2 tsp. (10 mL) soy sauce, sesame oil, ½ tsp. (2 mL) curry powder, chilies, garlic and ginger. Mix well. Let sit 20 minutes.
- To orange juice and reserved liquid, add cornstarch, 2 tsp. (10 mL) soy sauce and 1 tsp. (5 mL) curry powder. Stir well.
- Heat wok or large frying pan over medium-high heat, add oil. Stir-fry beef 2 minutes, add cauliflower and red pepper. Cook 4 minutes, add green onion. Cook 2 minutes more.
- Reduce heat to medium low. Add cornstarch mixture, cook and stir until thickened.
- Gently stir in orange segments, heat through.

Serve over steamed rice.

Yield: 4 servings
Serving Size 1½ cups (375 mL)
Preparation Time: 40 minutes

Nutritional Analysis
per serving

Calories	257
Protein	17.1 g
Carbohydrate	26.6 g
Fiber	3.8 g
Sugar	17.3 g
Fat	9.6 g
Cholesterol	40.8 mg
Saturated Fat	2.3 g
Mono Fat	4.7 g
Poly Fat	1.8 g
Folate	89 Ug
Vitamin C	113 mg
Sodium	449 mg
Potassium	675 mg
Iron	3 mg
Calcium	47 mg

Ginger Beef Kebobs

¼ cup	rice vinegar*	50 mL
¼ cup	soy sauce	50 mL
2 tbsp.	chopped cilantro	25 mL
1 tbsp.	sesame oil	15 mL
1 tbsp.	minced fresh ginger	15 mL
2	garlic cloves, crushed	2
½ tsp.	crushed chili flakes	2 mL
1 lb.	round steak, ¾" (2 cm) thick	500 g
16	medium mushrooms, wiped clean	16
1	green pepper cut into ¾" (2 cm) squares	1
4, 10"	skewers	4, 25 cm
¼ cup	honey	50 mL

- In a medium glass bowl, mix together rice vinegar, soy sauce, cilantro, sesame oil, ginger, garlic and chili flakes.
- Cut steak into 20 cubes approximately ¾ x 1 ¼ x 1¼" (2 x 3 x 3 cm).
- Toss meat in the marinade; cover and refrigerate a minimum of 2 hours or up to 8 hours.
- Alternately thread mushrooms, green peppers and meat onto skewers (reserve marinade).
- Add honey to marinade; bring to a boil and boil for 3 minutes (in microwave or on the stove).
- Place kebobs on barbecue over high heat or under broiler.
- Turn and baste twice during 10 minutes cooking time. Give the kebobs a final baste as they are removed from the barbecue.
- Do not over cook, meat should be medium rare.

* White vinegar may be substituted for rice vinegar.

Serve with steamed rice.

Yield: 4 servings
Serving Size: 1 skewer
Preparation Time:
  18 minutes

Nutritional Analysis
per serving

Calories	241
Protein	21.2 g
Carbohydrate	22.8 g
Fiber	.9 g
Sugar	20.4 g
Fat	7.2 g
Cholesterol	41.9 mg
Saturated Fat	1.9 g
Mono Fat	2.8 g
Poly Fat	1.7 g
Folate	22 Ug
Vitamin C	19 mg
Sodium	1067 mg
Potassium	471 mg
Iron	3 mg
Calcium	15 mg

Beef and Pepper Quesadillas

2 tsp.	canola oil	10 mL
1	red bell pepper, cut into ¼" (6 mm) strips	1
1	green bell pepper, cut into ¼" (6 mm) strips	1
1	small onion, slivered	1
6, 8"	tortillas	6, 20 cm
2 cups	thinly sliced roast beef cut into ¼" (6 mm) strips	500 mL
1½ cups	shredded Monterey Jack cheese	375 mL
	chili flakes (optional)	
	salsa	
	sour cream	

- In a medium frying pan, over medium heat, heat oil and sauté peppers and onion for 6 minutes.
- Remove from heat; divide into 6 portions in frying pan.
- Lay tortillas on a flat surface 2 at a time.
- Place ⅓ cup (75 mL) of beef on half of each of the tortillas.
- Spoon a portion of peppers and onions on top of beef.
- Top with ¼ cup (50 mL) grated cheese.
- Sprinkle with chili flakes to taste.
- Fold tortillas in half to form a semicircle.
- Heat a large frying pan over medium to medium-low heat. Wipe with canola oil to lightly coat.
- Place 2 quesadillas in the frying pan. Cook for 1½ minutes, or until golden brown. Flip over and cook 1½ minutes.
- Cut quesadillas in half crosswise on a serving plate.
- Repeat the process with the remaining tortillas.
- Serve each person 2 quesadilla halves with salsa and sour cream.

Yield: 6 servings
Serving Size:
  2 halves
Preparation Time:
  30 minutes

Nutritional Analysis
per serving

Calories	274
Protein	15.8 g
Carbohydrate	22.8 g
Fiber	1.8 g
Sugar	.9 g
Fat	14 g
Cholesterol	44.6 mg
Saturated Fat	5.8 g
Mono Fat	4 g
Poly Fat	1.8 g
Folate	12 Ug
Vitamin C	23 mg
Sodium	666 mg
Potassium	110 mg
Iron	2 mg
Calcium	249 mg

Barbecued Beef on a Bun

4 lb.	boneless beef cross rib or rump roast	2 kg
2	garlic cloves, sliced in half lengthwise	2
1 tbsp.	canola oil	15 mL
	salt and black pepper to taste	
¼ cup	thick barbecue sauce	50 mL
12	kaiser OR hamburger buns	12

- Preheat oven to 325°F (160°C).
- Place roast in roasting pan.
- Poke 4, ½" (1 cm) deep holes randomly in roast. Insert garlic halves in holes.
- Drizzle oil over roast.
- Sprinkle with salt and pepper to taste.
- Brush 2 tbsp. (25 mL) barbecue sauce over roast. Cover and bake for 3½ hours.
- Remove roast from oven. Let rest 30 minutes before slicing.
- Thinly slice the roast, piling meat into an 8-cup (2 L) casserole.
- Mix remaining barbecue sauce with pan juices.
- Pour over sliced meat. Cover and keep warm until serving.
- Pile ½ cup (125 mL) meat onto each bun.
- Garnish with condiments of your choice.

Serve with baked beans or Crispy Potato Wedges, page 116.

Note: Condiment suggestions include thinly sliced onion, dill pickle, horseradish sauce, mustard, chutney, etc.

Yield: 12 servings

Serving Size: 1 bun
Preparation Time:
  15 minutes

Nutritional Analysis

per serving

Calories	435
Protein	38.2 g
Carbohydrate	30.8 g
Fiber	1.4 g
Sugar	4.8 g
Fat	16.4 g
Cholesterol	84.1 mg
Saturated Fat	5.5 g
Mono Fat	6.2 g
Poly Fat	1.8 g
Folate	21 Ug
Vitamin C	1 mg
Sodium	443 mg
Potassium	648 mg
Iron	5 mg
Calcium	63 mg

Liver, Bacon and Onions

½ cup	milk	125 mL
1 tbsp.	soy sauce	15 mL
1 tbsp.	Worcestershire sauce	15 mL
1	garlic clove, crushed	1
1 lb.	sliced beef liver	500 g
4	slices bacon, cut in half	4
⅓ cup	all-purpose flour	75 mL
¼ cup	cornmeal	50 mL
½ tsp.	EACH paprika, seasoning salt	2 mL
¼ tsp.	granulated garlic	1 mL
¼ tsp.	black pepper	1 mL
1	medium onion, sliced	1

- In a 7 x 11" (17 x 28 cm) baking dish, combine milk, soy sauce, Worcestershire sauce and garlic.
- Cut liver slices to make 4 equal portions.
- Add the liver to the milk marinade; marinate for 1 to 8 hours in refrigerator.
- In a large nonstick frying pan, over medium-low heat, cook bacon 15 minutes, turning several times.
- While bacon is cooking, in a pie plate, combine flour, cornmeal, paprika, seasoning salt, garlic and pepper.
- Remove liver from marinade; discard marinade.
- Coat both sides of liver in the flour mixture.
- Remove bacon from frying pan and set aside. Fry liver slices in the bacon fat for 6 minutes, or until the top is wet. Turn over, laying onion slices on top. Cook for 6 minutes. The center of the liver should be just pink.
- Remove liver to warm serving plate. Keep warm.
- Continue cooking onions for 5 minutes, or until soft, stirring frequently.
- Arrange onion and bacon on liver.

Serve with Cheese and Herb Mashed Potatoes, page 115.

Yield: 4 servings
Serving Size: 1 piece
Preparation Time:
  1 to 8 hours for
  marinating,
  40 minutes prepara-
  tion

Nutritional Analysis
per serving

Calories	257
Protein	20.6 g
Carbohydrate	23.6 g
Fiber	1.6 g
Sugar	1.7 g
Fat	8.4 g
Cholesterol	290.7 mg
Saturated Fat	2.9 g
Mono Fat	2.6 g
Poly Fat	1.5 g
Folate	144 Ug
Vitamin C	21 mg
Sodium	510 mg
Potassium	372 mg
Iron	5 mg
Calcium	37 mg

DESSERTS

Healthy
Eating for
Healthy
Lifestyles

Ricotta Filling for Strawberries or Plums

½ cup	light ricotta cheese	125 mL
1 tsp.	lemon juice	5 mL
2 tsp.	honey	10 mL
½ tsp.	grated lemon peel	2 mL
2 tsp.	chopped fresh mint OR	10 mL
	½ tsp. (2 mL) dried	
12	large strawberries OR	12
	4 black plums	
	fresh mint leaves	

- In a small bowl, combine cheese, lemon juice, honey, lemon peel and mint until well blended. Refrigerate for 30 minutes.
- Scoop out blossom end of strawberries with a melon baller or grapefruit knife.
- Fill strawberries with 2 tsp. (10 mL) of cheese mixture.
- If using plums, cut plums in half, remove pit and scoop out a ball of flesh with a melon baller. Top with 1 tbsp. (15 mL) of filling.
- Garnish strawberries or plums with a mint leaf. Arrange on a serving plate.

Yield:
6 servings for strawberries;
8 servings for plums
Serving Size:
2 strawberries OR
1 plum half
Preparation Time:
45 minutes

Nutritional Analysis
per serving

Strawberries

Calories	36
Protein	1.8 g
Carbohydrate	4.9 g
Fiber	.6 g
Sugar	4.4 g
Fat	.9 g
Cholesterol	5 mg
Saturated Fat	.5 g
Mono Fat	0 g
Poly Fat	0 g
Folate	7 Ug
Vitamin C	15 mg
Sodium	19 mg
Potassium	50 mg
Iron	0 mg
Calcium	42 mg

Plums

Calories	39
Protein	1.5 g
Carbohydrate	6.6 g
Fiber	.5 g
Sugar	4.7 g
Fat	.8 g
Cholesterol	3.8 mg
Saturated Fat	.4 g
Mono Fat	.1 g
Poly Fat	0 g
Folate	3 Ug
Vitamin C	4 mg
Sodium	14 mg
Potassium	63 mg
Iron	0 mg
Calcium	30 mg

Mango-Pineapple Sorbet

1	mango*	1
1½ cups	water	375 mL
⅓ cup	honey	75 mL
8 oz.	can crushed pineapple	227 mL
¼ cup	freshly squeezed lemon juice	50 mL

- Peel and slice mango onto a baking sheet lined with waxed paper. Freeze.
- In a medium saucepan, combine water and honey. Bring to a boil over medium to medium-high heat.
- Remove from heat, add pineapple with juice and lemon juice. Stir and cool.
- Pour pineapple mixture into a container to freeze.
- When frozen, scoop out and place in a blender or food processor along with frozen mango slices. If ice and mango do not purée easily, let them sit for 5 minutes to warm up a bit, then try again.
- Purée until smooth and light in color. Freeze again.
- Use an ice cream scoop to scoop out sorbet.

* Fresh ripe mangoes are delicious, sweet, smooth and very juicy. When fresh mangoes are unavailable, canned mango pulp or slices make a good substitute.

Yield: 15 servings
Serving Size: ⅓ cup
 (75 mL)
Preparation Time:
 18 minutes

Nutritional Analysis
per serving

Calories	38
Protein	.2 g
Carbohydrate	10.2 g
Fiber	.4 g
Sugar	9.4 g
Fat	.1 g
Cholesterol	0 mg
Saturated Fat	0 g
Mono Fat	0 g
Poly Fat	0 g
Folate	3 Ug
Vitamin C	7 mg
Sodium	1 mg
Potassium	1 mg
Iron	0 mg
Calcium	5 mg

Orange-Berry Parfaits

4 tbsp.	custard powder	60 mL
⅓ cup	granulated sugar	75 mL
2½ cups	unsweetened orange juice	625 mL
2 tsp.	grated orange peel	10 mL
2 cups	fresh OR frozen blueberries OR mixed berries	500 mL
2 tbsp.	granulated sugar	25 mL
¼ tsp.	cinnamon	1 mL
	whipped cream OR vanilla yogurt to garnish	

- Measure custard powder and sugar into a saucepan or microwave-safe bowl.
- Gradually add orange juice, stirring to blend.
- Cook the custard and stir over medium heat until mixture comes to a boil or microwave on High for 6 to 9 minutes, stirring twice during cooking.
- Add orange peel.
- Cool for 30 minutes, stirring occasionally.
- In a bowl, combine berries with sugar and cinnamon. Let sit for 30 minutes.
- Spoon alternate layers of orange custard and berries into parfait or champagne glasses, beginning with custard and ending with berries.
- Top with a dollop of whipped cream or vanilla yogurt. Sprinkle with cinnamon.

Yield: 6 servings
Serving Size: 1 parfait
Preparation Time:
 45 minutes

Nutritional Analysis
per serving

Calories	138
Protein	.9 g
Carbohydrate	34.3 g
Fiber	1.9 g
Sugar	29.3 g
Fat	.4 g
Cholesterol	1.5 mg
Saturated Fat	0 g
Mono Fat	0 g
Poly Fat	0 g
Folate	49 Ug
Vitamin C	42 mg
Sodium	4 mg
Potassium	226 mg
Iron	0 mg
Calcium	15 mg

Fruit Pizza

½ cup	margarine, softened	125 mL
½ cup	brown sugar	125 mL
1	egg, beaten	1
1 tsp.	vanilla	5 mL
½ cup	all-purpose flour	125 mL
2 tbsp.	natural bran	25 mL
½ cup	quick-cooking oatmeal	125 mL
¼ cup	unsweetened fine coconut	50 mL
½ tsp.	baking soda	2 mL
½ cup	light cream cheese	125 mL
1 cup	no-fat lemon yogurt	250 mL
	assortment of fresh fruit*, e.g., sliced banana; strawberries; seedless grapes halved; peeled, sliced kiwi, mandarin orange segments, etc.	
1 cup	pineapple juice	250 mL
1 tbsp.	cornstarch	15 mL

- Preheat oven to 350°F (180°C).
- In a bowl, combine margarine, brown sugar, egg and vanilla. Stir well to blend.
- In a separate bowl, combine flour, bran, oatmeal, coconut and baking soda. Add to the margarine and sugar mixture. Mix well.
- Spread over a 12" (25 cm) pizza pan that has been lightly sprayed with nonstick cooking spray.
- Bake for 10 to 12 minutes. Cool.
- In a deep bowl, with an electric mixer, blend together the cream cheese and yogurt until smooth. Spread over cooled crust.
- Arrange the fruit in a circular pattern to completely cover the top of the pizza.
- In a saucepan, mix pineapple juice with cornstarch. Cook over medium heat until it comes to a boil and is thickened, stirring constantly.
- Spoon glaze over fruit to cover, filling any gaps.
- Chill for 3 hours before serving.

Yield: 12 servings
Serving Size: 1 slice
Preparation Time:
  40 minutes

* Nutrient analysis is for 1 cup (250 mL) EACH of watermelon, honeydew, strawberries, kiwi, pineapple, grapefruit.

Nutritional Analysis
per serving

Calories	211
Protein	3.8 g
Carbohydrate	25.4 g
Fiber	1.3 g
Sugar	15.6 g
Fat	10.7 g
Cholesterol	23.1 mg
Saturated Fat	3.3 g
Mono Fat	3.3 g
Poly Fat	3.1 g
Folate	14 Ug
Vitamin C	12 mg
Sodium	230 mg
Potassium	200 mg
Iron	1 mg
Calcium	57 mg

Chocolate Crêpes with Bananas

Crêpes

½ cup	all-purpose flour	125 mL
¼ cup	cocoa	50 mL
¼ cup	granulated sugar	50 mL
4	eggs	4
½ cup	1% milk	125 mL
2 tbsp.	unsalted butter, melted	25 mL
2 tsp.	canola oil	10 mL

Custard Sauce

4 tsp.	custard powder	20 mL
4 tsp.	granulated sugar	20 mL
1¼ cups	1% milk	300 mL
2	large bananas	2
2 tbsp.	unsalted butter, softened	25 mL
2 tbsp.	brown sugar	25 mL
1 tsp.	vanilla	5 mL
1	dark chocolate bar OR milk bar chocolate OR baking chocolate square	1

- To prepare the crêpes, in a blender or food processor or with a whisk, combine flour, cocoa, sugar, eggs, milk and melted butter. Blend well.
- Cover and let batter sit for 1 hour at room temperature, longer in the refrigerator.
- In an 8" (20 cm) nonstick frying pan, heat 2 tsp. (10 mL) of oil to coat the frying pan well.
- Scoop ⅓ cup (75 mL) of batter into the frying pan. Swirl to coat pan; pour excess batter back into bowl.
- Cook crêpe until no wet spots appear on top, about 30 seconds.
- Loosen edges; flip crêpe over. Cook other side briefly, about 10 seconds.
- Remove crêpe from pan. Repeat with remaining batter, lightly oiling pan as needed.

Chocolate Crêpes with Bananas

Continued

- To prepare the custard, in a saucepan, combine custard powder and sugar.
- Slowly add milk, stirring to blend.
- Cook and stir over medium heat until mixture comes to a full boil. Remove from heat.
- Peel bananas, slice in half crosswise then again lengthwise.
- In a medium frying pan, over medium to medium-low heat, melt butter with brown sugar.
- Add bananas and vanilla; toss to coat. Cook for 2 minutes, turning occasionally.
- Reduce heat to low and cook for 3 minutes.
- Lay a crêpe flat. Place a banana half on top, roll up crêpe, tucking in sides. Repeat with the remaining crêpes.
- Lay crêpes on dessert plates; pour 2 tbsp. (25 mL) of sauce over each crêpe.
- Grate chocolate over crêpes to garnish.

Note: Crêpes can be stacked one on top of the other. If crêpes are being made a few days in advance, then stack with waxed paper between crêpes. Wrap well; refrigerate or freeze for longer storage.

Yield: 8 servings (8 Crêpes)

Serving Size: 1 crêpe
Preparation Time:
 45 minutes

Nutritional Analysis
per serving

Calories	195
Protein	6.2 g
Carbohydrate	28.8 g
Fiber	.9 g
Sugar	18 g
Fat	6.3 g
Cholesterol	117.4 mg
Saturated Fat	3.1 g
Mono Fat	2 g
Poly Fat	.5 g
Folate	22 Ug
Vitamin C	3 mg
Sodium	69 mg
Potassium	262 mg
Iron	1 mg
Calcium	88 mg

Blueberry Banana Whip

2 cups	crushed graham wafers	500 mL
⅓ cup	butter OR margarine, melted	75 mL
3 cups	frozen blueberries	750 mL
2½ tbsp.	cornstarch	30 mL
¾ cup	granulated sugar	175 mL
1 cup	whipping cream	250 mL
¼ cup	icing (confectioner's) sugar	50 mL
12 oz.	light quark	340 g
2	bananas	2
2	kiwi fruit to garnish	2

- Preheat oven to 350°F (180°C).
- In a bowl, combine crushed wafers and melted butter. Mix well.
- Pat into an 8 x 12" (20 x 30 cm) ovenproof pan. Bake for 12 to 15 minutes, until golden brown. Cool
- Cook blueberries with cornstarch and sugar in a medium saucepan over medium heat until thick and clear.
- Remove berries from heat; cool for 45 minutes.
- In a bowl, beat cream, gradually adding icing sugar, until stiff.
- In a medium bowl, fold quark and whipped cream together.
- Spread half of the cream mixture over the crumb crust.
- Slice bananas over top.
- Spread a layer of blueberries over the bananas, then the rest of the cream mixture.
- Refrigerate for 2 to 4 hours.
- When ready to serve, slice fresh kiwi over each serving.

Variation: Substitute chocolate wafers or ginger snaps for graham wafers.

Yield: 12 servings
Serving Size: 1, 3 x 3"
  (7.5 x 7.5 cm) piece
Preparation Time: 1
hour

Nutritional Analysis
per serving

Calories	303
Protein	6 g
Carbohydrate	42.1 g
Fiber	2.6 g
Sugar	25.5 g
Fat	13.4 g
Cholesterol	28.1 mg
Saturated Fat	6.5 g
Mono Fat	2.6 g
Poly Fat	.6 g
Folate	12 Ug
Vitamin C	15 mg
Sodium	144 mg
Potassium	176 mg
Iron	1 mg
Calcium	28 mg

Baked Pineapple Sundae

1	pineapple	1
¼ cup	liquid honey	50 mL
2 tbsp.	butter	25 mL
1½ cups	frozen vanilla yogurt	375 mL
2 tbsp.	low-fat chocolate sundae topping	25 mL
6	strawberries	6

- Preheat oven to 375°F (190°C).
- Cut the top from the pineapple. Peel, core and cut the pineapple into 6 long spears.
- Place the pineapple spears in a row crosswise in an 8 x 12" (20 x 30 cm) baking dish.
- Drizzle with honey and dot with butter.
- Cover the baking dish tightly with foil wrap. Bake for 20 to 30 minutes, until hot and bubbly.
- Cool for 15 minutes.
- Top each spear with ¼ cup (50 mL) of frozen yogurt.
- Drizzle each spear with 1 tsp. (5 mL) of chocolate topping and 1 sliced strawberry.

Yield: 6 servings
Serving Size: 1 sundae
Preparation time:
  6 minutes

Nutritional Analysis
per serving

Calories	197
Protein	2.1 g
Carbohydrate	34 g
Fiber	1.2 g
Sugar	24.6 g
Fat	7.1 g
Cholesterol	12.3 mg
Saturated Fat	4.3 g
Mono Fat	1.8 g
Poly Fat	.4 g
Folate	13 Ug
Vitamin C	20 mg
Sodium	87 mg
Potassium	193 mg
Iron	0 mg
Calcium	61 mg

Broiled Oranges

2	large oranges	2
2 tsp.	packed brown sugar	10 mL
2 tsp.	soft butter	10 mL
½ tsp.	rum (preferably dark) OR ¼ tsp. (1 mL) rum extract OR vanilla	5 mL
dash	cinnamon	dash
	blueberries, fresh cherries OR mint leaves for garnish	

- Preheat broiler.
- Cut oranges in half crosswise.
- With a grapefruit knife or serrated knife, cut along rind and membranes to separate pulp as you would a grapefruit. Leave orange pulp in rind as in a "bowl".
- In a small bowl, combine sugar, butter, rum and cinnamon.
- Spread ½ tsp. (2 mL) of sugar mixture over each orange.
- Place orange halves in a 7 x 11" (17 x 28 cm) baking dish.
- Broil oranges 4 to 5" (10 to 12 cm) from the heat for 2 to 4 minutes, or until hot and bubbly.
- Top with berries, cherries or mint leaves. Serve immediately.

Serve with thin wafer cookies such as chocolate, spice or almond wafers.

Dessert

Warm Berry Sauce on Yogurt Cups,
page 202

Yield: 4 servings
Serving Size: ½ orange
Preparation Time:
  10 minutes

Nutritional Analysis
per serving

Calories	60
Protein	.7 g
Carbohydrate	11 g
Fiber	1.7 g
Sugar	8.3 g
Fat	2.1 g
Cholesterol	5.5 mg
Saturated Fat	1.3 g
Mono Fat	.6 g
Poly Fat	.1 g
Folate	21 Ug
Vitamin C	37 mg
Sodium	22 mg
Potassium	135 mg
Iron	0 mg
Calcium	31 mg

Baked Apples with Apricots

4	baking apples*	4
¼ cup	chopped dried apricots	50 mL
4 tsp.	chopped pecans	20 mL
2 tsp.	butter	10 mL
1 tbsp.	packed brown sugar	15 mL
dash	cinnamon	dash

- Preheat oven to 350°F (180°C).
- Wash and core apples.
- With a sharp knife, score a line around the middle of each apple.
- Place apples in a baking dish.
- Fill apple cavities with 1 tbsp. (15 mL) of chopped apricots and 1 tsp. (5 mL) of pecans.
- In a small bowl, cream together butter, brown sugar and cinnamon.
- Divide butter mixture evenly among the apples, topping each cavity.
- Bake in the center of the oven for 45 minutes.
- Place apples in serving dishes and drizzle any juice left in the baking dish over them. Serve.

* Good baking apples include Granny Smith, Northern Spy, Ida Red, Baldwin, Winesap, Cortland, Golden Delicious and Rome Beauty.

Yield: 4 servings
Serving Size: 1 apple
Preparation Time:
 12 minutes

Nutritional Analysis
per serving

Calories	174
Protein	1.1 g
Carbohydrate	35 g
Fiber	5.4 g
Sugar	28 g
Fat	4.9 g
Cholesterol	5.5 mg
Saturated Fat	1.5 g
Mono Fat	2.1 g
Poly Fat	.8 g
Folate	7 Ug
Vitamin C	8 mg
Sodium	24 mg
Potassium	409 mg
Iron	1 mg
Calcium	22 mg

Poached Pears Stuffed with Camembert Cheese

2 cups	cranberry OR cranberry blend juice	500 mL
½ cup	granulated sugar	125 mL
2"	piece of stick cinnamon	5 cm
1	(½ x 2" [1.3 x 5 cm]) strip of orange peel	1
4	whole cloves	4
1 tsp.	vanilla	5 mL
4	firm Anjou pears	4
2 oz.	Camembert cheese, quartered	60 g
¼ cup	finely chopped toasted pecans, almonds OR walnuts	50 mL

- In a large stainless steel saucepan or Dutch oven, combine cranberry juice and sugar until dissolved.
- Add the cinnamon stick, orange peel, cloves and vanilla.
- Bring to a boil, over medium heat, reduce heat and simmer for 5 minutes.
- Meanwhile, peel pears with a vegetable peeler, leaving stems on.
- Cut a thin slice off the bottom of each pear to create a flat base so the pear will stand upright in the poaching liquid. Place pears upright in the simmering poaching liquid.
- Cover and cook over low heat, basting occasionally for 20 to 25 minutes, or until the pears are tender but firm.
- Remove pears with a slotted spoon. Place them on their sides on paper towel to drain and cool.

Poached Pears Stuffed with Camembert Cheese

Continued

- Over medium-high heat, bring the poaching liquid to a boil; heat to a slow boil.
- Reduce liquid to ⅔ cup (150 mL) of syrup.
- Remove and discard cinnamon stick, orange peel and cloves.
- Pour syrup into a container; refrigerate for 15 minutes, or until it has thickened.
- While syrup is cooling, use a melon baller to remove a 1" (2.5 cm) core at the base of each pear.
- Fill each cavity with 1 piece of cheese.
- Brush the base and 1" (2.5 cm) along the bottom side of each pear with syrup.
- Sprinkle 2 tsp. (10 mL) of nuts onto the glaze.
- Arrange pears upright on a dessert plate, brush tops with syrup. Spoon syrup on the dessert plate, around the base of the pears.

Yield: 4 servings
Serving size: 1 pear
Preparation Time: 1 hour

Nutritional Analysis
per serving

Calories	431
Protein	7.6 g
Carbohydrate	75.8 g
Fiber	6.1 g
Sugar	62.7 g
Fat	13.4 g
Cholesterol	10.2 mg
Saturated Fat	2.8 g
Mono Fat	3.2 g
Poly Fat	6.2 g
Folate	34 Ug
Vitamin C	37 mg
Sodium	122 mg
Potassium	383 mg
Iron	1 mg
Calcium	93 mg

Nutrition Tips:

After a sports event or exercise, there is some evidence that muscle glycogen is restored faster if you include some protein with your recovery carbohydrates. Bread or a bagel with some cheese is a good suggestion.

Pear and Cherry Crisp

4	large Anjou pears, peeled, cored, quartered and quarters sliced crosswise (4 cups [1 L])	4
⅓ cup	dried cherries	75 mL
⅓ cup	apple juice	75 mL
¼ cup	granulated sugar	50 mL
1 tbsp.	lemon juice	15 mL
1 tbsp.	instant tapioca	15 mL
¾ cup	granola	175 mL
½ cup	all-purpose flour	125 mL
⅓ cup	lightly packed brown sugar	75 mL
¼ cup	margarine, melted	50 mL

- Preheat oven to 350°F (180°C).
- In a bowl, combine pears, cherries, apple juice, sugar, lemon juice and tapioca.
- In another bowl, combine granola, flour, brown sugar and margarine. Blend well until crumbly.
- Lightly spray an 8" (2 L) square baking dish with nonstick cooking spray.
- Spoon pear mixture into the baking dish.
- Sprinkle granola mixture over.
- Bake for 1 hour, or until the top is a deep golden brown and the juice is clear and bubbling.

Variations: Fruit crisps are easy and delicious. Use your favorite fresh fruit in season and include dried fruits if you wish. Good flavor combinations are rhubarb and strawberries, peaches or nectarines and blueberries, apples and cranberries or blueberries or raisins. A sprinkle of cinnamon adds good flavor to the apple or peach versions.

Yield: 6 servings
Serving size: ¾ cup (175 mL)
Preparation time: 15 minutes

Nutritional Analysis
per serving

Calories	343
Protein	3.4 g
Carbohydrate	62.5 g
Fiber	3.9 g
Sugar	35.4 g
Fat	10.5 g
Cholesterol	0 mg
Saturated Fat	3 g
Mono Fat	3.4 g
Poly Fat	3.4 g
Folate	22 Ug
Vitamin C	6 mg
Sodium	137 mg
Potassium	324 mg
Iron	2 mg
Calcium	43 mg

Caramel Apple Pudding

This pudding makes its own luscious caramel sauce – an easy recipe with a high comfort quotient.

2 cups	diced apples	500 mL
1 tbsp.	lemon juice	15 mL
1 cup	all-purpose wheat and oat flour	250 mL
2 tsp.	baking powder	10 mL
2 tsp.	granulated sugar	10 mL
¼ tsp.	salt	1 mL
2 tbsp.	butter	25 mL
½ cup	milk	125 mL
¼ cup	chopped pecans	50 mL
1 cup	Demerara sugar OR brown sugar	250 mL
1½ cups	boiling water	375 mL
2 tbsp.	butter	25 mL
1 tsp.	ground ginger	5 mL

- In a bowl, mix diced apple with lemon juice. Set aside.
- Preheat oven to 375°F (190°C).
- In a medium bowl, combine flour, baking powder, sugar and salt.
- Cut in butter with a pastry blender until crumbly.
- Add milk, diced apple and pecans. Stir until just blended.
- Turn into a deep 6-cup (1.5 L) casserole that has been sprayed with nonstick cooking spray.
- In a bowl, combine Demerara sugar, boiling water, butter and ginger. Stir well.
- Pour sugar mixture over pudding. Do not stir or cover.
- Bake for 40 minutes, or until golden.

Yield: 6 servings
Serving Size: 1 cup
(250 mL)
Preparation Time:
20 minutes

Nutritional Analysis
per serving

Calories	374
Protein	4 g
Carbohydrate	66.8 g
Fiber	4.5 g
Sugar	46.6 g
Fat	12.2 g
Cholesterol	23.3 mg
Saturated Fat	5.6 g
Mono Fat	4.4 g
Poly Fat	1.3 g
Folate	13 Ug
Vitamin C	5 mg
Sodium	328 mg
Potassium	364 mg
Iron	2 mg
Calcium	190 mg

Warm Berry Sauce on Yogurt Cups

Frozen berries make this sauce a snap. The flavor is very fruity and the color is gorgeous.

Warm Berry Sauce

2 cups	frozen mixed berries (strawberries, blueberries, blackberries, raspberries)	500 mL
1 cup	cold water	250 mL
2 tbsp.	cornstarch	25 mL
⅓ cup	granulated sugar	75 mL
1 tsp.	vanilla	5 mL
	cinnamon	
	vanilla yogurt	
	sponge cake dessert cups	

- In a medium saucepan, combine berries, water, cornstarch and sugar. Cook over medium-high heat for 6 minutes, stirring occasionally until the sauce comes to a boil.
- Reduce heat to medium-low, keeping a slow simmer. Cook for 3 minutes, until sauce is clear and thickened.
- Remove sauce from heat. Stir in vanilla and cinnamon. Let cool to just warm.
- Place a dessert cup on a serving plate. Top with ¼ cup (50 mL) of yogurt. Spoon ¼ cup (50 mL) of warm berry sauce over top.

Variations: Substitute a scoop of frozen vanilla yogurt for the vanilla yogurt. Garnish with fresh berries if desired. Leftover sauce can be stored, covered, in the refrigerator. Use on angel food cake, ice cream, pancakes, French toast, waffles, etc.

Pictured on page 195.

Yield: 8 servings

Serving Size: ¼ cup (50 mL) of sauce
Preparation Time: 20 minutes

Nutritional Analysis

per serving

Calories	72
Protein	.3 g
Carbohydrate	17.9 g
Fiber	1.6 g
Sugar	13.4 g
Fat	.1 g
Cholesterol	0 mg
Saturated Fat	0 g
Mono Fat	0 g
Poly Fat	.2 g
Folate	9 Ug
Vitamin C	7 mg
Sodium	2 mg
Potassium	50 mg
Iron	0 mg
Calcium	8 mg

Vanilla Pound Cake with Yogurt Sauce and Fruit

½ cup	butter, softened	125 mL
1 cup	granulated sugar	250 mL
1 tsp.	vanilla	5 mL
3	eggs	3
1½ cups	all-purpose flour	375 mL
1 tsp.	baking powder	5 mL
¼ tsp.	salt	1 mL
½ cup	no-fat plain yogurt	125 mL

Yogurt Sauce

1½ cups	no-fat plain yogurt	375 mL
2 tbsp.	brown sugar	25 mL
1 tsp.	rum extract	5 mL
½ tsp.	vanilla	2 mL
	fresh berries, peaches, etc. for garnish	

- Preheat oven to 350°F (180°C).
- Grease and flour a 3 x 5 x 9" (7.5 x 13 x 23 cm) loaf pan.
- In a bowl, beat butter with sugar until blended.
- Add the vanilla and the eggs. Beat for 30 seconds on medium speed, scraping bowl. Beat on high for 3 minutes, scraping bowl occasionally.
- Beat in flour, baking powder, salt and yogurt until blended. Pour batter into the loaf pan.
- Bake for 65 to 70 minutes, or until a toothpick inserted in the center comes out clean.
- Cool for 10 minutes; remove from pan to cooling rack. Cool completely.
- In a bowl, combine yogurt, brown sugar, rum extract and vanilla. Cover and refrigerate.
- At serving time, spoon 2 tbsp. (25 mL) of yogurt sauce onto a slice of cake. Garnish with berries or sliced fruit.

Variation: ⅓ cup (75 mL) of raisins, plumped in warm water and well drained, may be added to the yogurt sauce.

Yield: 12 servings
Serving Size: ¾" (2 cm) slice
Preparation Time: 15 minutes

Nutritional Analysis
per serving

Calories	245
Protein	5.4 g
Carbohydrate	34.5 g
Fiber	.4 g
Sugar	20.8 g
Fat	9.5 g
Cholesterol	74.8 mg
Saturated Fat	5.5 g
Mono Fat	2.8 g
Poly Fat	.5 g
Folate	15 Ug
Vitamin C	0 mg
Sodium	207 mg
Potassium	133 mg
Iron	1 mg
Calcium	116 mg

Pumpkin Pie

This pumpkin pie is crustless, for less work and fewer calories, a win/win combination.

3	eggs	3
¼ cup	margarine, melted	50 mL
1 cup	1% milk	250 mL
1¾ cups	cooked, puréed pumpkin OR 14 oz. (398 mL) can	425 mL
⅔ cup	brown sugar	150 mL
½ cup	fine unsweetened coconut	125 mL
½ cup	all-purpose flour	125 mL
1 tbsp.	pumpkin pie spice	15 mL

- Preheat oven to 350°F (180°C).
- In a blender, combine eggs, margarine, milk, pumpkin, brown sugar, coconut, flour and pumpkin pie spice. Mix well.
- Pour into a 9" (22 cm) pie plate, lightly sprayed with nonstick cooking spray.
- Bake for 50 to 55 minutes, or until a knife inserted in the center comes out clean.
- Cool and refrigerate. Serve with a dollop of whipped cream and a sprinkle of cinnamon.

Yield: 8 servings
Serving Size: ⅛ pie
Preparation Time:
  10 minutes

Nutritional Analysis
per serving

Calories	239
Protein	5 g
Carbohydrate	33.1 g
Fiber	2.1 g
Sugar	21.9 g
Fat	10.2 g
Cholesterol	80.7 mg
Saturated Fat	3.7 g
Mono Fat	3.2 g
Poly Fat	2.5 g
Folate	20 Ug
Vitamin C	3 mg
Sodium	141 mg
Potassium	278 mg
Iron	2 mg
Calcium	85 mg

Date Turnovers

Date Filling

1 lb.	pitted dates	500 g
¼ cup	water	50 mL
2 tbsp.	lemon juice	25 mL

Turnover Dough

2 cups	all-purpose flour	500 mL
2 cups	quick-cooking rolled oats	500 mL
1 cup	granulated sugar	250 mL
½ tsp.	EACH salt, cinnamon	2 mL
1 cup	shortening	250 mL
½ cup	1% milk	125 mL
1 tsp.	lemon juice	5 mL
1 tsp.	baking soda	5 mL

- To prepare filling, on a cutting board, with a large sharp knife, chop dates.
- Place dates in a microwave-safe bowl with water and lemon juice. Cover; heat on Low for 5 minutes, until softened. Stir to break up. Cool
- To prepare dough, in a medium bowl, combine flour, rolled oats, sugar, salt and cinnamon. Cut in shortening.
- In a small bowl, stir together milk and lemon juice. Add baking soda and stir to dissolve.
- Add enough milk mixture to the flour mixture to make a dough that can be rolled out on a lightly floured surface.
- Preheat oven to 350°F (180°C).
- On a floured surface, roll dough to ⅛" (3 mm) thick. Cut with a 3" (7.5 cm) round cookie cutter.
- Spoon 2 tsp. (10 mL) of date mixture onto each round. Fold in half; seal edges with a fork.
- Bake on a baking sheet for 15 to 18 minutes, until light brown.
- Cool on a baking sheet for 5 minutes. Remove to a cooling rack.
- When cool, pack into airtight containers. Allow turnovers to sit 24 hours to soften.

Yield: 40 servings (40 turnovers)

Serving Size: 1 turnover
Preparation Time: 60 minutes

Nutritional Analysis

per serving

Calories	269
Protein	3.3 g
Carbohydrate	42.1 g
Fiber	2.8 g
Sugar	25 g
Fat	10.4 g
Cholesterol	.2 mg
Saturated Fat	2.6 g
Mono Fat	3.4 g
Poly Fat	2.6 g
Folate	9 Ug
Vitamin C	1 mg
Sodium	126 mg
Potassium	200 mg
Iron	1 mg
Calcium	30 mg

Index

Desserts

Fish & Meat Dishes

Glazes, Salad Dressings, Sauces, Seasonings & Toppings

Lunches At Home & Portable

Portable Snacks

USA Swimming Fun Facts

- 1984 – Nancy Hogshead and Carrie Steinseifer tie for the gold medal in the 100m freestyle in the first race of the Olympics. It's the only tie in Olympic swimming history.

- The same firm that erected the St. Louis Arch installed the flume, which was recognized as one of the Seven Engineering Wonders of the Year in 1989.

- 1990 – *Sports Illustrated* names Mary T. Meagher's 200m butterfly world record (1981) as the fifth-greatest "single-event" record ever.

- In both the 1992 and 1996 Olympics, USA Swimming's athletes represented ¼ of all medals won by all American athletes. 1996 marked the first time that swimming out-medaled track and field.

- Plato considered a man who didn't know how to swim uneducated.

- In the 1920s, Johnny Weismuller set world records in 67 different events. In his 10 years of amateur swimming, he never lost a race. However, he was best known for his role as Tarzan on the big screen.

- At the first modern Olympic Games in 1896 only freestyle events were held. In 1900 a backstroke event was added, followed by breaststroke in 1904 and butterfly in 1956. Women swimmers did not compete in the Olympics until 1912.

- Throughout her career, Tracy Caulkins held numerous world and American records. Considered by many to be the greatest swimmer of all time, she is the only swimmer ever, man or woman, to own American records in every stroke.

- In 1926, Gertrude Ederle became the first woman to swim the English Channel. Her time of 14 hours and 34 minutes broke the men's record for the crossing.

- The night before the 400 IM finals in the 1964 Olympics, Dick Roth was stricken by an attack of appendicitis but refused an operation. He swam the event, winning a gold medal.

- In 1972, Mark Spitz became the first man to win seven gold medals in one Olympics, all in world record times.

Stand on Shore or Make a Ripple

- Since 1896, the United States has won 400 medals in swimming competition, including 177 gold medals. No other country has won more than 123 total or 53 gold medals.

- Since 1985, USA Swimming's athletes have set world records on 65 separate occasions.

Fitness Swimmer (Aug/Sept 98)

	Body Weight			
	130	150	170	190
Swimming	Calories Burned Per Minute			
Backstroke	10.0	11.5	13.0	14.5
Breaststroke	9.6	11.0	12.5	13.9
Butterfly	10.1	11.7	13.2	14.2
Freestyle, fast	9.2	10.6	12.0	13.4
Freestyle, slow	7.6	8.7	9.9	11.0

Splash! (July 93)

- At the Pan Pacific Championships in 1989, American swimmers broke four world records in a period of 6½ hours.
  - Mike Barrowman – 200m Breaststroke (2:12.89)
  - Janet Evans – 800m Freestyle (8:16.22)
  - Dave Wharton – 200m IM (2:00.11)
  - Tom Jager – 50m Freestyle (22.12)

USA Swimming

Swimming is one of the most popular sports in America, and for every one of the more than 250,000 people who participate in it each year, there's a personal reason why swimming is his or her sport of choice. Some want to participate in the Olympics. Some want to challenge themselves by achieving new goals. But most just want to make friends and have fun.

Isn't it time you said "yes" to a lifetime of fun, fitness and friendship?

To become a member of USA Swimming, please contact your local swim club.

More information on USA Swimming and the name of the swim club nearest you can be found on the USA Swimming web site at **www.usa-swimming.org**